THE BUILDING OF AN IDEAL FAMILY

SAYED H. ROHANI

TABLE OF CONTENTS

41. <u>AMBIGUITY TOWARDS THE UNIVERSAL TRAITS</u>

42. <u>WHAT IS TIME?</u>

1

THE BUILDING OF AN IDEAL FAMILY

The desire to enjoy an ideal family is an absolute intuition, but to idealize this desire is an insurmountable mission. This is the dream of every parent to establish a family being sound, healthy, and prosperous as much as possible. It is understandable that parents' dream of building such a family will be out of commission unless they make sacrifices to build one. First and foremost, they themselves must be good parents and worthy of parenthood; that is, they had better be model parents to inspire their children and family members practically, not just verbally. A father who is unfaithful to his wife cannot impress their children by advising them to be faithful to their spouses. A father who trespasses on people's rights cannot teach their children lessons of honesty. Or a father who is prone to excessive indulgence cannot invite their children to moderation. However, they may change their negativity into a positive attitude by making an attempt to atone for past wrongs, leaving their undesirable ventures behind, and regretting their misdeeds. Furthermore, parents should warn their offspring against their own improper experiences they have suffered from to prepare their sons and daughters for future aright and to inculcate good habits in them. Establishing a strong bond between parents and children is crucial. Proper communication and presence of parents with their children are likewise imperative. It is also important to know how and with whom their children spend time.

Each family is a brick of its society, and society is made of these bricks. Therefore, the stronger and sounder these bricks, the healthier the society. The building of an ideal family cannot be achieved by empty talks. It needs sound direction, secure commitments, firm determination, a strong mind, great soul, and a marvelous heart. The following seven items are tailored to build healthy families everywhere, at all times:

Love: Love is the light of every family. A house where there is no love, there is no light, suffering from frigid cold and pitch dark. Love between parents conveys a warm and insightful message to their children. As a strong rope, love connects the family so cohesively that it will save them from disintegration. A loveless

marriage will lead to parents' dissolution, inflicting a blow upon the entire family. What is unholy about love is to mix it up with lust and thus vitiate its value. Let's hear of Victor Hugo, "Life is the flower for which love is the honey." Aristotle is more serious about love, "Love is composed of a single soul inhabiting two bodies."

Loyalty: If love is the light of a household, loyalty is the magic to sustain and strengthen the relationship between husband and wife, inspiring them to be open with one another, encouraging them to pour out their heartstrings, giving them the opportunity to discover each other's dilemmas, and empowering them to combat any bane impairing their relationship. Loyalty between parents passes a great message to their offspring. Loyalty should come from both husband and wife. If one of them tears apart the tenet of loyalty, their marriage will fall apart, so that it will end in divorce. Thus, disloyalty has induced myriads of divorces, and loyalty has kept marriages intact.

Leadership: When we think of leadership, we usually envisage big political, social, or educational establishments and governments. In fact, leadership can be incorporated into the first society, the smallest social unit, such as a family, too. The first society, the smallest social unit, a family is quite compatible to be tailored to meet the criteria to be entitled to leadership, policies, and polity. Although politics is not compatible with a family due its abuses and corruption, leadership and policies are vital for a family. As a smallest organized unit of society, a family can function as a polity. The more a family enjoys good leadership, the more it runs by harmony, solidarity, education, and wisdom. A good leadership will not only keep a family solidified, well-educated, comfortable, and economically successful but also encourages universal values, such as justice, virtue, faith, goodness, good ethics, and decorum; inspiring children with good books cultivating a superb mind, good heart, and great soul. Once again, education must be the topmost priority. Family members should be convened time after time to issue advice, discussing policies and values, identifying and warning against what is wrong and harmful, elaborating policies, and making sure that whatever is advised should be practiced. These policies and advice will cover from small activities such as using a toothbrush and toothpaste to the most intricate moral, sociological, psychological, and philosophical topics and discussions. Sound leadership creates discipline, creativity, solidarity, broad education and knowledge, sound directions, effective directive, beneficial strategies to make life beautiful and easy.

Leniency: Most of the time, tiny and trivial issues induce big dilemmas between husband and wife, so that sometimes even ending up in divorce. The more the parents are critical of one another and cavil at the issues, the more the problems will multiply. It is best to be lenient to each other, not only towards small issues but also as to the serious problems. To be forgiving and lenient toward each other creates optimism and discourages negativism, carping, and worrying. In fact, leniency gives children freedom to develop their abilities and intuition without restraint. Martinetish behavior is a negative concept, keeping creativity and intuitive abilities down. Sound leadership not only brings peace and warmth in the family, but also establishes practical plans on how to leverage the resources. Economic failure is an influencing factor in tearing apart the tenet of the families. Reduced circumstances will give rise to chasm between parents, which may lacerate the entire family relations if families are morally incompetent, given to secular life, lacking in patience and strength, and whose pride goes before a fall. To combat this situation, we need to do three things: first, we should endure it with fortitude; second, we are to work ethics by using the entire efforts of the family efficiently to generate income to relieve the financial difficulty; third, we should leverage the present resources as much as we can to make both ends meet; that is, to stick to the basic necessities and economize to the best possible way. To furnish a family with ethical and moral inspirations is the business of sound leadership. Moral ideas prompt peace, dignity, and discipline. There is liberated life and so is libertine life: they are like two prisons—external and internal. Of course, an external prison whereof we are all acquainted is a physical establishment for the prisoners. But there is also one inside us called libertine prison wherein are held immoral people who are given to licentious, depraved, and degenerate desires. In fact, mostly people who are in the external prisons have been first inmates of their internal prisons. Immorality is the intoxication of the soul, victory of the devil. The more our soul is intoxicated, the more we are given to overindulgence. Therefore, a liberated life is free from both of these prisons; a libertine life is actually enslaved by licentious desires. To be liberated suggests to be in charge of our lives, in control of our desires, and cognizant of our choices. Immorality vitiates our harmony, tarnishes our hearts, and impairs human nobility. Once we are in the hands of uncontrollable desires, we trespass the tenet of family sanctity, and we will behave so irrationally that the helm of family will swerve from its original course so much so that the family disintegration will be necessitated.

Education is an imperative issue to be clearly and   strongly highlighted by the family leadership. Education experience is great life exploration. Family leadership plays an important role to inculcate ideal education in the family. Several important factors should be considered in the matter of education. Family members' talent, taste, and skills should be discovered and to improve them proper steps should be taken, wise decisions should be made. Education not only turns per se into a great source of livelihood, it also creates business, craft, career, and skills that provide a family with plenty of economical success. In addition to economic success, it brings about social, political, and psychological   triumph. In the past, education was a privilege just for the elite, but in the passage of time, it started to become a widespread ideal. Now all the people: the rich, the poor, the weak, and the strong aspire to benefit from it. In truth, parents who are aware of educational opportunities, encourage education first and foremost.

Cooperation is a blessing phenomenon to instill in a family. It creates love, comfort, and good relationships between the family members, encouraging their self-esteem. I have seen a lot of families who have been deprived of the sense of cooperation have been torn apart. Cooperation between the parents strengthens the foundation of the family. Children are affected by their parents in multiple ways. Children usually model themselves on their parents, learning good and bad habits from them. Conflict between parents creates a lot of tension, giving rise to discomfort, disturbing the peace. This situation may induce a negative effect on the children's life. Family cooperation brings happiness to the members on the one hand, and nourishes optimism, autonomy, and confidence on the other, even to deal with the outside problems.

Faith is so significant that it should have been discussed first, but it came last to be remembered by the readers to be used as a cohesive wrap to bunch up all other ideas in this essay. It will allow us to know right from wrong, to recognize both our weak and strong points, and to strengthen the weak points. It will warn against what is negative, preventing us from committing evil things. A lucid faith fortifies us with trust, truth, respect, dignity, and resilience; stopping us from vulgarity; and encouraging good habits. Faith is a serious issue. It does not play cheaply, vulgarly, or erroneously. It always takes matters seriously. It never lies or falsifies. It smiles, but it never smiles fakely. Thus, when people of faith promise something, they are inspired by their faith to be obligated to carry their promise. Therefore, they are people of commitment, encouragement, values, discipline, and consistency. Faith invigorates spiritual growth, inspiring positive values. While love connects husband and wife and other members of a family, faith will maintain and solidify this connection. Without faith, loyalty loses its way. In fact, faith liberates one from wrong choices, urges against wrong ways, and encourages what is good, beautiful, and virtuous.

2

THE PURSUIT OF AN IDEAL LIFE: AMITY BETWEEN THE TRIAD

Human beings are a combination of body, mind, and spirit. Therefore, those three elements should be recognized and managed properly. It's important to know how they interact and cooperate, and how they disintegrate and degenerate. The more harmony exists between the three, the better. Harmony involves a great sacrifice and real struggle, and faith is the stepping-stone to this harmony.

Humans are dominated by complex phenomena. Sometimes emotion is influenced by thoughts, and sometimes thoughts by emotion. In both ways, humans are exposed to deception and corruption, because true feelings are buried in the heart and the tongue speaks what is wrought and manufactured in the head, which defies the heart. At other times, emotion defies the thinking phenomenon or the logical organ of human beings, leaving it corrupt, naïve, and compromised. Emotion can be strong and overwhelming, as it may disrupt the logical network to remain at the helm. Sometimes emotion becomes so violent that it drives the person insane, so that he or she turns to anxiety, panic behavior, and even self-annihilation. To face the danger of such emotion, it is necessary that the person should recognize unhealthy emotion in order to take control, lest he or she be left at its mercy. How? That is the core of the problem. If you discover it, you seize it and control it. But, as a matter of fact, it shuns you—it hides and disguises itself under names and phenomena that seem to be legal and in conformity with standards of behavior. As it is true that a person without emotions is no more than a dead body, so is a person driven by emotion equally exposed to harm. It's also a good idea to remember that we cannot rely on our thoughts, either, for sometimes they may follow the path of evil. As William James says, 'A great many people think they are thinking when they are merely rearranging their prejudices.' Accordingly, if neither emotion nor thoughts can be trusted, you may wonder what the alternative may be. In fact, any kind of extremism is wrong unless it can somehow lead to perfection. The golden mean is the best to follow: for example, hope is the mean between despair and audacity; or choose the mean between frugality and miserliness. In the same way, as an emotional person is abnormal, so is an apathetic one. When you rationalize, you use facts and data, which are intellectual perspectives; when coming from emotional perspectives, you make use of your feelings and sentiments. Usually these feelings and sentiments are expressed through your heart. That is why your true feelings are expressed by your heart if they are not disguised and influenced by thoughts.

Daniel Goleman has extensively researched the emotional sphere of the brain, or LeDoux has painstakingly researched how the systems in the brain work— especially, his valuable information on fear. If so, how can that information mislead a good number of people? I've no intention of disparaging their important work; however, I've certain remarks on Goleman's *Emotional Intelligence*.

In the first place, Goleman's brain research is highly scientific; therefore, it needs special effort and understanding to grasp. In the second place, his style of writing is so appealing and intriguing that his entire work appears to ensure consistency and is tailored to prove his points adequately. But a critical view of his work proves that his ideas are flawed and inconsistent. First of all, it is emotional and dicey to talk about *emotional intelligence*. Goleman's and others' finds about the mind, compared to the treasures already created by the human mind, are like a drop in the ocean. I mean Goleman brags about brain research as if it's the best source of information. But the human mind has already done wonders: think about literary and artistic works such as poems, novels, plays, epics, operas, music, paintings, sculptures, drawings, architectures, etc.; think of social sciences such as psychology, economics, political science, anthropology, and sociology; think of natural sciences such as physical sciences, earth sciences, life sciences, each of which can be subdivided into an array of disciplines; think of diverse mental abilities to plan, to experience, to question, to interpret, to formulate, to guess, to assess, to judge, to project, to conclude, to solve, to create, to invent, to decide, and so forth—these and myriad other things are activities of the mind.

There are events that cannot be calculated or assessed by researchers, and will fail the brain research. Faith, spirituality, belief, and religion work wonders. It's faith that reconciles emotion and cognition and makes use of volition to serve them with honesty and loyalty. A good heart works better than an intelligent mind, or a good heart may perceive better than an intelligent mind. Look at those people who have been very educated—perhaps they have graduated from the most prestigious universities, or those who claim to be the brains of the people—they have entered human society to serve the people, but instead they have done great disservices to them and have been disposed to commit egregious acts. Perhaps they bribe or extort; they are arrogant; they think of their own advantage and care not a straw for others; they jeopardize others' rights and liberty, toy with others' welfare and happiness, impose themselves upon others, impose their will on others; they deceive and lie; they satiate their ugly desires; they booze and lust after women; they mock, disparage, despise, and are ungrateful; they put their needs above others'; they abuse and use others to serve their vicious desires; they ignore others, they break their promises, they misjudge…and they commit many other wrongs. What is wrong with them? Aren't they who claim to be cultured and civilized, with their minds cultivated, sufficiently educated? Aren't they sufficiently intelligent to live a decent life?

Think of those who have been raised in a family devoid of humanity and understanding, entering society with nothing but ugly manners; or think of those who have been deprived of caring parents, deprived of educational and social opportunities, and deprived of those means to live proper lives. Do we accept their malicious deeds and ugly attitudes because of their deprivation? Do we accept their malevolence because they have been deprived of good parents and proper opportunities to fulfill their needs, to accomplish and succeed properly? And now think of those who have been deprived of prestigious colleges, deprived of social and economic opportunities, and in the face of all their problems, they are humble, do not steal, are patient, do not show a bad attitude, do not take revenge, do not harm; they struggle to succeed, use the right sources to navigate their barriers, and are determined to be good and do good. In the light of these instances, what do you think will lead the people into goodness? Enough intelligence? Wealth? Prosperity? Social success? Or what will lead them into evil? Poverty and privation? Peer and environmental pressures? Hardship?

Sometimes people think that poverty and privation will lead into evil; intelligence and prosperity will lead to goodness. If it were so, all the poor and needy would be evil people, and all the intelligent and prosperous would be good people. I believe there is a very intricate relationship among emotional, cognitive, and volitional functions. Sometimes people follow their emotions, and other times they are influenced by their cognition, and volition always follows the orders of the function that is more influential, whether that be the emotional or cognitive sphere.

How does volition follow the orders of the one that is more influential? Volition is just like a soldier who takes orders only from the powerful. Suppose that one's heart is set on robbing a bank. His volition is directed toward that goal despite all the dangers, difficulties, and barriers. Or one is set to save a life. His volition will be directed toward that aim despite imminent dangers and difficulties.

To be sure, by emotions I mean anger, contempt, disgust, fear, embarrassment, helplessness, worry, doubt, envy, frustration, shame, sadness, despair, hurt, courage, hope, pride, satisfaction, trust, stress, shock, tension, calm, content, amusement, excitement, pleasure, joy, lust, love, friendliness, interest, politeness, surprise, suffering, neglect, and so forth. By cognition I mean thinking or reasoning power, including critical thinking. By volition I mean the faculty of using one's will or willpower. Although the triad lives under the same roof, they are not necessarily in harmony and in peace. Sometimes they are; sometimes they aren't. The underlying causes of their imbalance can be naïveté and weakness of mind, or violence of the emotional domain. As I said, volition accepts the orders of the one that is dominant and superior. There are also underlying causes for cognitive weakness and for emotional violence. As a matter of fact, cognitive dominance will not always lead to positive outcomes, nor will emotional dominance always lead to results. How? To answer this question, I have to retract my argument and ask you if educated people are always fine, truthful, helpful, and good? To be sure, there are two kinds of uneducated people: good and bad. The same is true of educated people. Now we are of the same opinion: Educated people rob in daylight, in suits; uneducated people in the dark, in rags. Educated people use their sophisticated and highly developed minds, high-tech systems and strategies, highly developed plans and procedures. In fact, the late-2000s financial crisis was the product of highly educated minds, a product of emotional dominance. What is emotional dominance? Sometimes the human heart becomes so perceptive, so intuitive, that it overshadows the activities of the mind.

You may think that while I am questioning emotional intelligence in the first place, how I am talking about the perception and intuition of the heart. That's a very good point. I have two explanations for your answer: First, although the emotional domain of the mind perceives the information from the outside, either its perception can be flawed, or its response—or both. How? For example, when the emotional domain is affected by sadness, it can neither accurately figure out the source of sadness, nor can properly provide a solution to defuse or soften it. Therefore, it turns to the realm of thought for help. For example, suppose the emotional domain is affected by sadness, it cannot ascertain its source: it could be somebody's death, loss of money, loss of property, imprisonment, any kind of failure, and myriad other causes. Also, it does not know how to provide a suitable answer: if, for example, the cause is death, how to comfort; if it is imprisonment, how to achieve release; if loss of money, how to gain it back; if failure, how to correct it, and so forth.

My next explanation is associated with spirituality, the invisible that makes things visible, the unknown that makes things known, and the alien that explains mind-numbing things. It's spirituality that gives significance to morality and conscience. Conscience is the faculty that can recognize right from wrong. It is spirituality that polishes and inspires the emotional domain of the mind, giving rise to humanistic qualities such as love, kindness, tolerance, patience, empathy, charity, mercy, forgiveness, goodwill, and magnanimity. As an immaterial, eternal reality, spirituality is enjoyed by all those who are in pursuit of inner peace, happiness, and hope; who aspire to connect themselves to God, the divine realm, and sublime experiences; who are in search of faith, truth, sublime love and beauty, and creativity; and who are walking with fortitude, living with certainty, defending truth, and considering the criteria of right and wrong. I wonder how brain researchers such as Goleman balance thought with emotions. I am convinced that emotion not only fails to balance thought, but also creates chaos in the realm of thought. Why? Because it's the thinking realm that suffers the ravages of emotions. Think of those whose rational minds have been blasted by *lust*, and who have committed rape and murder and other mayhem; think of those whose rational minds have been overwhelmed with *pride* and *triumph* and have left multitudes dead; think of those whose rational minds have suffered from *anger* and have risked lives and property; or think of those whose thoughts have been ravaged by *envy*, which has had dangerous results…and there are many more such examples. As I explained, it's spirituality that gives harmony not only to emotion, but also to cognition. Why do you think those who are highly educated are committing heinous crimes? Why do their highly developed thoughts fail to prevent them from wrongdoing? It's because they are lacking spirituality.

To expand my discussion, spirituality brings harmony and reconciliation between cognition and emotion, enlightening them with humanity. Inspired by faith and spirituality, the human mind, with cognition at the helm, functions properly. The relationship between emotions and thought will be established in the best possible way. Thoughts will think right, and emotions will be under control. All the emotional components will carry out their responsibilities in a proper manner.

To give a true picture of the human mind, I'd like to add that intricate relationships are established not only between the cognitive, emotional, and volitional domains of the mind, but also between the components of the emotional domain itself. These components team up either to wage a war, or to make peace. *Fear*, although it appears to be a negative component and often the person who fears is put to shame, may also be useful. For example, *fear*, which teams up with its peers such as horror, anxiety, alarm, worry, distress, powerlessness, hopelessness, and such, is used as a restraint against pride, triumph, hope, and courage, which may create mayhem; it also protects against lust, desire, and passion, which tear all the chains apart to hold the torch of pleasure; it also stands against anger, disgust, and irritation, which trigger negative results. As you see, all the emotional components are working together in this manner. However, in the absence of spirituality, they transgress their limits and revolt against the power of thought; facing the threat, cognition is left confused, and thus it will ultimately surrender to emotion. But when emotions are inspired and illuminated by spiritual light, they become so caring and friendly that they are ready to give a sacrifice as a good-will gesture."

I remember once I witnessed an incident in which the above-mentioned sacrifice was made. A couple of poor workers were working in a village, on sheep and goat intestines, cleaning them, freeing from fat. They were working for an export company. I believe the animal intestines are used for stringed instruments, as in Shakespeare's verse: 'Is it not strange that sheep's guts should hale souls out of men's bodies?' To resume my story, there was a deep ditch, seemingly unsecured, where the waste was thrown. One day one of these workers slipped into the ditch, and he was drowning in the waste. His coworker dropped himself into the ditch to save him. In a short while both of them died. This is an example of a pure act of love and caring. You may impugn his act as a reckless worker, arguing he could have saved his friend and himself if he had used his mind. Pure love and sacrifice override and outwit the mind. There are many examples of love that, in order to reach its goal, ignores all kinds of orders, navigating the seven seas, negotiating impassable boundaries, and undertaking unthinkable tasks. A true love ascends to heaven; lust and desire descend into chaos.

How spiritually inspiring it is to see the stars shine in the clear, blue sky! How lovely to see and hear the waves! How delightful to be on top of a cliff and look below into the river murmuring into the grass, all green and beautiful, and into the trees, the quiet of nature! How it is inspiring to be all alone once in a while! I don't discourage you from being with others; however, it's essential to be alone now and then to think about your accomplishments, to reflect on your actions, to examine your thoughts and feelings, to explore your mistakes in order to correct them, to review your regrets in order to learn from them, and to confess your sins and ask forgiveness from Almighty God. How lovely and beautiful it is to meditate, to communicate with God! You feel calm, relaxed, comfortable; you feel as if your burdens have been unloaded, your soul lightened, your responsibilities shouldered or completed. You'll come to understand the true meaning of such meditations when you're stuck in a difficult, critical, life-and-death situation; for example, suppose you're deep underground, alive, but you've no exit to get out. Think of Captain Falcon Scott and his four companions who lost their lives in the blizzards during their expedition to the Pole. Or think about the thirty-three Chilean miners who were 2000 feet below the ground, captive for sixty-eight days.

If you encounter an accident so that your cruise is on the verge of being drowned, whom would you think of? Do you think of a rescuer, of your relatives, or of death? What if no soul can rescue you but God? In our lives, once in a while, we'll encounter catastrophes in the sea, in the air, or on the ground, so that we'll be left completely alone, and no soul can help us. Then, you can't help but think of God, trust in God, the depth and foundation of spirituality, and thus you are indeed in pursuit of an ideal life, which is clear of the traps of beguiling time; life, which aspires to perfection, to happiness, and to harmony; life, which is clear from the evil path.

3

WHAT IS THE HEART OF HUMANITY?

Have you enjoyed a charitable heart? Have you devoted yourself to a great cause? Have you saved a life? Have you risked your life to rescue somebody from a certain danger or affliction? Have you commiserated with the afflicted? Have you alleviated the hurt? Have you dried the tears of orphan children, listened carefully to their stories, and served their wishes? Have you protected the poor from the cold winters and hot summers? Have you provided the homeless with shelters? Have you served the underserved, the disadvantaged? Have you catered to the needy sick with medical care? Have you sought the safety of those powerless and hopeless fallen into the wrong hands? Have you assisted the poor? Have you taken care of the needy? Have you given food to the hungry, water to the thirsty? Have you brought a cessation to hostilities? Have you brought peace to the warring parties? If you have, in fact, you are a man or a woman of compassion. Compassion is the heart of humanity, and you are a part of this heart, because all those charitable acts contribute to humanity.

Compassion is the most beautiful reality, the most magnificent quality of heart, whose beauty encircles human with a halo of light enjoying such a healing agent that inspires people with goodness, transforming them into charitable mortals, and turning their deeds worthwhile. It is through compassion that we find forgiveness and blessing, that we are trusted for friendship, that we enjoy peace and serenity and admiration, that we build relationships and harmony, and that we congratulate ourselves on humanity.

If passion makes you wild and woolly, compassion calms you down, touching you with a touch of humanity, preparing you to purify your heart, purge your soul, refine your mind, and humanize your personality. Coming from the depth of heart as an enlightening phenomenon, compassion benefits all as a great friend, serving all with utmost charm and nobility, without consideration of mercenary motives.

Compassionate feelings are so balanced, peaceful, holy, and serene that they make the heart feel good, the soul feel great, and the mind could be endowed with such ability to live in conformity with the feelings, feelings with such transparency could be distinguished from the negative ones.

When you wish to have your prayers granted, when you are prepared to admit your wrongs and ready to regret, when you clean up your acts and purge yourself from sins, when you are getting off your high horse, when you break up with cruelty and soften your heart, when you supplicate to get rid of your pains or afflictions, when you are prepared to change for the better, you appeal to compassion and humility. Compassion is the entrance into humanity.

4

IS THERE A DIFFERENCE BETWEEN VICTIMS AND CRIMINALS? ARE VICTIMS AND CRIMINALS CONCLUDED EVENLY?

This question: "Is there a difference between victims and criminals?" may seem to be so obvious that nobody, nowhere, at any time, will expect to hear it, and nobody will care to think about it to provide an answer for. In the face of all this obvious perception, I have raised this question, and I am convinced that there is a multitude of people who are not convinced of making distinction between the two practically; however, they may believe that there is a manifest difference between the victims and criminals theoretically. Who are they? Actually, they are those who believe that death is the end of everything, that both good deeds and misdeeds have no significance after one dies, that criminals go unpunished, and good people go unrewarded. Thus, in the wake of death, serial killers or saints, tyrants or kindhearted ones, rapists or the raped, criminals or victims, are the same, regardless of what they were and what they did. This idea is rampant among the atheists, agnostics, cynical or skeptical individuals, and those who are theists theoretically but not practically. This idea elaborates that those who have spent their time in corruption have the same share as those spending time doing good. Those who are murdering are the same like those who are saving lives. Or the award of those who give charity is counted similar to that of those who rob the people's property. Generally speaking, the distinction between those two categories will be clouded or lost if we think that as soon as they die, their cases are wrapped up permanently.

In the face of law, of course, a definition between law-abiding citizens and lawbreakers has been established, so that the criminals are prosecuted and their punishment is calculated by the severity of their crime. However, there have been a lot of instances where criminals have escaped the punishment. For example, they have been on the loose, or they may have been replaced by an innocent person mistakenly, or they may have been exonerated by obstruction of justice, nepotism, or any other ways. Thus, we see that law has not always been perfectly practiced, and therefore criminals could have escaped it. To conclude, it is not the perfect standard to be able to deal with every single criminal. As a matter of fact, justice will only be perfect and immaculate when every single criminal is punished according to his or her crime.

If you work for someone the whole day, and you are refused to receive your wage at the end of the day, how do you feel? Don't you feel that you are mistreated, oppressed, ripped off, or deprived of what is yours? Certainly, you do. And aren't you different from those who have spent their day futilely? Certainly, you are. This truly happens when the efforts of those who have spent their life usefully are gone by the wind as soon as they die. If so, aren't they similar to those who have lived lavishly out of the robbery? If death will be the end of all things, then the party who have lived lavishly out of the robbery have had better luck than those who have spent time doing good. If so, their goodness has not been paid off at all. In theory, it is believed by everyone that good deeds are good and useful only in this life. There are people who believe that good deeds continue to pay off the life after, but there are also many who think good deeds are good only in this life, not in the life after, because they do not believe in the after life. Thus, it is safe to say that they only in theory believe that good deeds are good because they are useful, though they do not benefit from them financially. Those who believe in the life after, they practically believe that good actions are practically paid off by God by offering a heaven full of food and fruit and other facilities and services to fulfill our desires. The manner God pays off the good deeds is practical, being at odds with a multitude of people who consider these good deeds only theoretically, insignificantly, nominally.

In the same way that there is a purpose for creation, so is for sickness, health, poverty, failure, etc. If creation belongs to a well-founded design, everything that has been created makes sense. If there are things that we cannot make sense of, in fact, our mind is short of their understanding, even if there are happenings that involve loss of lives, disasters, and diseases. In the same way that the universe is governed by fixed laws, our actions and behaviors are also geared to follow a path that is right and proper, and deviation thereof means transgression. Thus, right and wrong conducts are created, and so are their rewards and retributions. If good deeds go unrewarded, they are reduced to nothing: a work unpaid, an attempt failed, or a battle vanquished.

Human is not a dish to be broken and left in oblivion as meaninglessly as its broken pieces, nor a recipe to be eaten and lost in the stomach inconsequentially, nor a footprint to be lost and forgotten, nor a sea wave to appear and disappear momentarily, nor a leaf falling off the tree that eventually dissipating and desiccating, nor a pebble on the seashore. Human beings are intelligent, decent, conscientious, and responsible creatures to serve a purpose. As they are vested with intelligence, soul, and dignity, they are accountable for their actions, behavior, and decisions. Their deeds, good or bad, will not be lost, and they are consequential.

Are you convinced that there is justice and law and order and tenets among human beings, creatures of God, but not in the kingdom of God? What makes you come to such a belief? What about those crimes that have escaped human justice either by neglect, or by prejudice, or by nepotism? What about the crimes having been committed against humanity in the course of history? What about the crimes that have never been made public?

And now do they who have spent time and efforts helping humanity expect nothing? What about those who have given sacrifices for the sake of humanity? What about those who have sacrificed their lives to save lives? What about those who have struggled to be good and to do good to bring justice, beauty, harmony, and wisdom? All their time, efforts, and sacrifices of no avail?
Do you think it makes sense that the first group who are composed of criminals should go unpunished, and the second group who are good people should go unrewarded? Do you think the whole universe is made out of nonsense so that no distinction should be made between good and bad, humanity and inhumanity, sacrifices and grudges? Do they both go on the same boat destined to the same fate and destination? Do you think this universe is a jungle guarded and run by the mindless?

In the same manner that nature changes by wearing different seasonal clothes, displaying its childhood, youth, and old age by means of color, human beings also go through different stages of life. Their lives involve various changes, colors, and meanings. Abundance and poverty, health and sickness, pain and suffering are few phenomena they encounter in the course of, accompanied with various challenges, escapades, experiences, and opportunities, and failures. The way the spring gives strength to the earth to revive, youth brings energy to life. The way winter stores the earth with water, old age prepares life with what is vested in it. Poverty similarly pushes life into new challenges, or for example, pain gives life new perspective and understanding. Thus, all these experiences fill up life with meaning and value and insight.

In fact, God's table of rewards is beyond our imagination and expectation. Fairness and generosity are two important elements of the table. To be awarded with these rewards, our work is not compared to what we do on earth, and we are repaid by our bosses and masters. God's injunctions are easy to perform, but His reward is very big. His reward is based on truthfulness, honesty, simplicity, goodness, and purity, being freed from any deception, trick, hypocrisy, corruption, prejudice, and other ugly aims and plans.

Every single action including good and bad will go in our record. Nothing will be erased, twisted, or changed. Do you think human misdeeds causing innocent people pain and miseries will get off scot-free? Do you think these misdeeds are footprints, waves of the ocean, raindrops, or bird droppings not to be accounted for? God's sovereignty is complete and perfect, with ultimate justice and fairness: the smallest goodness will not be left unnoticed and unrewarded.

5

THE GRAND ENTERPRISE

I recently learned that Jennifer Lopez received $1.75 million for a 40-minute private concert she performed for a family of casino magnates in Macau. There are similar examples that we waste a substantial fortune to indulge our fancies, while real causes that save humanity are given a damn. I want nobody to think that I am envious of those wealthy people who wish to spend their money the way they want. Do not even suspect that I would feel a twinge of envy for them. I'd better envy those noble acts that can survive me to be blessed with eternally, rather than such mundane, short-lived, transitory temptations and escapades. In fact, I am mentioning the Jennifer Lopez deal not out of envy, but out of other deeper thoughts encompassing such vital, humanitarian ideal that may overshadow feelings of envy, pride, or ambitions; dominating aspirations that knock at the door of humanity, and shaking up the conscience of the unconscious and unconscionable. This is a spiritual consideration, a philosophical deliberation, a deliberation necessitating the shakedown of our system and order of humanity, prompting a more profound reflection and reconsideration.

It goes without saying that there is a huge discrepancy among humankind in terms of wealth, ambitions, desires, and wishes, which is normal and legitimate. This discrepancy has been and will be in effect in the world of human beings. However, what makes this discrepancy abnormal when it is justifiable to admit that the fortune the family in Macau spend for just less than an hour to indulge their fancy can build thousands of shelters for the poor and homeless, save thousands of lives, brighten up thousands of faces, cheer up thousands of hearts, etc. Yes, everyday fortunes are spent on vanities, while great moral causes are being abandoned.

Wealth, sex, desires, and craze for popularity are the most established, flamboyant heritage of humankind. As grandest players, they have had the power, charisma, and the ruse to rule the people, enslaving them, fooling them, charming them, and taking them by surprise. They have not only brought distinction among the people, but they have also influenced the people's personality and disposition and have transformed them tremendously. The fever of sex, fame, wealth, and power has been so dominant and transformative that it has driven the people like dry leaves and thrown them like a ball. As a most powerful stimulant, it has put their lives in jeopardy, disgracing them, depraving them, and making a joke out of them. As a persuasive catalyst, it has played double agent. On the one hand, it has subdued, seduced, and sedated the people to drive them out of their senses. On the other hand, it has enkindled such motion and emotion in mankind that they have began to commit the wildest things, pursuing the most sensational things, committing the most dangerous things, risking their lives, playing with their lives, selling their souls for a petty trade, and exerting the most relentless efforts for popularity.

Yes, sensation of fame, sex, wealth and power has dragged the people into such a maze of escapades that they have gone berserk, pursuing their wild pursuits, trespassing the borders of safety, heading the perilous, unpredictable wilds. It has acted as sedatives obscuring people's eyes, capturing their hearts, confusing their minds, weakening their souls to make them dance to its tunes. Have you seen the ropewalkers crossing the Grand Canyon or Wheel of Death could be sent to death by a single misstep, a wave of mental confusion or wind? Have you seen the skydivers jumping from air balloons floating from some 120,000 feet above the earth to break the speed of sound in free fall? Have you seen the daredevil climbers whose claim to fame come only when climbing the tallest building such as Burj Khalifa without safety equipment? Have you seen those daredevils driving rocket-powered racecar at the speed of more than 618 miles per hour? Have you seen the daredevils jumping the Snake River Canyon on a motorcycle, dicing with death? When these daredevils perform these audacious stunts, I am not envying their fame and honor; I concern myself with their jeopardized lives. If you call these people ambitious and aspirant, then what about those who are given to greed, to pride and prejudice, to savagery, to murder spree, to rape, to child molestation, to robbery, to fraud, to deceit, to conspiracy, to wickedness, to abuse of power, and to many other crimes that have infested the human society? Haven't they gone astray by their wild whims and desires? Indeed, wishes that have been left unsupported by a healthy mind will follow a dicey future.

In fact, the daredevils buy fame and honor by putting their lives on the line; the pleasure seekers brave the exciting mazes and games; and the rich season their lives, boost and enrich their excitements by indulging their wild desires. Thus, two kinds of safety have been violated: moral safety, bodily safety. Moral safety is violated when moral values are laughed off and ignored. Morality protects an individual from detrimental plans and measures as does the towers protect a citadel from enemy's invasions. When morality weakens, mental power begins to erode, allowing all kinds of subversive ideas to invade the mind.

When mental power is compromised, life's security is also left on the line.

Pleasure of the flesh has always been working hand in glove with fancies and desires that sedate the senses, excite the feelings, charm the mind, induce self-indulgence and egotism, to pursue unhealthy whims. Although transitory and short-lived, these feelings mean so much to the people that they are deemed as precious as genuine and eternal phenomena, while being not more
than a deceptive mirage that shines as brightly as authentically from a distance, but, in reality, they are a temporary cloak of deception that obscure the minds of the people to winnow their way through ruses. Even if the reality of these caprices is betrayed, still they may influence and sedate the mind so much that the former, in the first place, undermines this realization, and in the second place, even with this realization, the matter will not be taken seriously.

As a matter of fact, desires are susceptible to many dangers, baits, and ruses, and our feelings are liable to them anytime and anywhere. If these feelings are abandoned by themselves and failed to be supported by a strong mind, they will be prone to a lot of changes and will be drawn here and there by mere fancies or inconsequential things.

How can we harness our desires to be a token of inspiration, not desperation? Don't you think this is a great enterprise? Don't you call it an achievement? You do spend effort and even a mint for all other undertakings to succeed, why not for this enterprise, which is the mother of all other enterprises? Yes, this enterprise, like all other projects, needs efforts, perhaps grander efforts for this one, which is the greatest enterprise—to harness our desires.

We have to work for it; we have to be moral and spiritual: this is the heart of the enterprise.

Morality and spirituality do not come by wishing upon stars. It involves cleaning one's soul, one's heart, and one's conscience. It needs to take from oneself and give to others. It means to become selfless, charitable, and magnanimous; it means to serve God and humanity from the depth and sincerity of heart: this is how we build the greatest enterprise, an enterprise that comes from purity and faith and will stay forever.

In contrast to the pleasures of the flesh, spiritual perspective comes to be noble, bona fide, eternal, and universal, and profound. Its world is free from deception, manipulation, reservations, obscurity, disharmony, unfairness, vanity, villainy, vulgarity, profanity, regret, miseries, jeopardy, etc. Its reward is according to good deeds, regardless of color, race, rank, power, and wealth.

The same criterion is used for everybody.
Spirituality involves balance, positivism, reason, nobility, virtue, health, felicity, perpetuation, righteousness, honor, truth, transparency, and other good and positive things. That is why everybody feels safe and secure in this realm. It does not involve extravaganza such as risking one's life, going nowhere or extreme, committing dangerous or illogical things, or wasting health or property unreasonably and inconsequentially. It is neither extreme nor short. It always defends the golden mean. Sometimes religious people get fanatic, committing dark deeds and ascribing them to spirituality. In truth, their perpetrations not only lack spirituality, but they can be subversively demonic. Spiritual deeds are usually peaceful, noble, veracious, harmonious, virtuous, and felicitous.

Parity, and disparity, rich and poor, dark and light, hardship and comfort, health and sickness, happiness and misery, good and bad, ugly and beauty are eye-opening phenomena. They have been created for real purpose, in due measure for the purpose of trials and signs for the wise. How the rich spend their wealth. Do they help the poor and fulfill the good causes, or do they waste to indulge their wild desires, take care of the wild fancies and escapades, or turn into a Korah? How the poor react against poverty and hardship. Do they suffer their pain with patience and nobility or become a rebel like Satan against God? By looking at the ugliness, we should appreciate the beauty, be patient against hardships, and cherish the ease.

If evil is substituted for good, if a straight path is traded for a crooked one, if a moral way is rejected for an immoral one, if dark thoughts are preferred to bright ones, there is certainly something wrong with our choices and ways of thoughts: this is a common sense, and it needs to be addressed to build the grand enterprise to deliver and exalt our souls and serve humanity.

6

THE HEART OF KNOWLEDGE

Do you know what the heart of knowledge is? Perhaps everyone thinks the heart of knowledge will be the catalyst leading one to happiness. True, the heart of knowledge induces universal, absolute, and perpetual happiness. Do you know what this knowledge is and what kind of knowledge will lead you to happiness?

People are learning knowledge for several reasons. Those who want to be teachers are studying pedagogical skills and facts. Those who want to be doctors are studying medical stuff. Those who want to be engineers try to study engineering sciences. Those who want to be an auto mechanic are learning mechanicals. So do the carpenters, the goldsmiths, the cobblers, the watchmakers, the nurses, the hairdressers, etc. are learning things related to their business. They learn their business to become successful in what they do. Their success involves not only satisfying their own needs and ambitions but also the needs of their society. They take advantage of their knowledge to get hired, and they get hired to sell their knowledge to maintain their lives. They exploit their knowledge in two ways: either they work for the people, and they are called hires, or they work for themselves. Selling one's skills to maintain life is one way of dealing with one's knowledge. This enables us to socialize and be a part of the working members of the society. There is also

19

another way to enjoy knowledge: to acquire knowledge to nourish one's own mind and soul without taking advantage out of it commercially. Growth of mind and soul is a great spiritual ambition, which overshadows those ambitions that are desired materially, because the former serves the spirit, the latter the body.

Spiritual growth is desired to feel happy and great. Usually, spiritual growth is different from material growth. Spiritual growth provides us with a beautiful heart, great conscience, exquisite mind, and healthy personality. Material growth, which satisfies our worldly ambitions and wishes, sometimes becomes so unruly that it bars spiritual growth from expansion.

As we mentioned, knowledge is used either for material comfort or spiritual happiness. In fact, both businesses are looked after to bring about happiness. Therefore, happiness is the ideal of all. First of all, it is wise to first define what happiness is and then go after it. If we define happiness as pleasure, prosperity, joy, comfort of life, well being, and freedom from pain, then everyone has his or her own definition and explanation for happiness. A sick person who has just left a terrible illness behind will feel very happy, or a prisoner who has completed a sentence is very jolly, or a homeless person who has owned his or her first shelter will enjoy one of a kind happiness. Give a hungry man or woman a platter of food; in fact, how happy he or she will feel! Now think about a rich man who has become poor—how does he feel? He will feel so miserable that he will loathe his life. Similarly, if we lose one of our offspring, how will we feel? Won't we feel sad? Won't we feel frustrated when we fail a task, lose a campaign, or lose a job? In the light of all these instances, we come to understand that happiness comes and goes, or even if it stays a little longer, it still seems to be vulnerable to time and other conditions that are beyond our control. In this case, happiness seems to be a relative concept varying among individuals. There are people who feel happy after they have suffered misery, and they have come to a realization and knowledge. Perhaps this happiness may ring truer than the one that materially achieved. In fact, such phenomena as miseries, misfortunes, or problems churning out happiness involve an internal change that may lead to a formidable change that can be permanent or stay longer.

By what we have understood, we realize that the meaning of happiness changes in terms of its duration. To be happy for a week is better than being happy for a day, or to be happy for a month is better than being happy for a week, or to be happy for a year is better than being happy for a month. Thus, the longer we are happy, the better. Therefore, a person who lives a lifelong comfort and ease will feel to be the happiest man, though life is not free from trouble and tears.

We concluded that we learn and acquire knowledge to be comfortable, and pursuit of happiness is our ideal. We acquire knowledge to give meaning to life, to discover life, and to find out what real happiness is. Happiness is not something to be bound by time because happiness is timeless, eternal. Happiness does not come by wealth because there are many wealthy people who are not happy, and wealth is not a medium of happiness. What if you are wealthy but unhealthy? Happiness does not come from pleasure because pleasure is not a medium of happiness, too. We might smile with pleasure for sometime, but that time ends, and so does your pleasure.

So how can we avail ourselves of true happiness, which is eternal, which is not bound by time and material, and which lives with us forever? How? Happiness is one of the universals such as truth, justice, goodness, humanity, and so forth, which is not subject to decadence and perishing. In the same manner that we exert ourselves to be crowned with truth, justice, goodness, and humanity, we also strive to attain eternal happiness. We have to struggle to earn it. In the same way that we struggle for material enjoyment, we also need to strive for happiness. To obtain material benefits, we can use machinations and fool others or ourselves. As about happiness, it does not work that way. We have to be true crusaders; we have to be honest, truthful, and good to enjoy eternal happiness. Now we raise the question—how can we succeed in pursuing an eternal happiness? As we discussed, we pursue knowledge either for material comfort or spiritual enjoyment. We mentioned that material comfort comes to an end, but spiritual enjoyment stays with us forever, beyond the time. Now we have to search for the knowledge that leads us into eternal happiness. This knowledge is unique; that is why it is the heart of knowledge: it is the heart of knowledge because it makes us eternally happy and prosperous.

Knowledge that brings us happiness is the heart of knowledge. Where does this knowledge come from? It comes from God—The One, The First, The Last, All-Wise, All-Knowing, All-Hearing, All-Seeing, All-Powerful, The Manifest, The Most High, The Everlasting, The Unfailing, The All-Forgiving, The Self-Subsisting Sustainer of All, The Self Sufficient, The Loving, The Glorious.

Without this knowledge, happiness is a pure imagination. It is in the light of God that all universals such as truth, goodness, humanity, justice, etc., are realized, and so is true of happiness. To know God is not a mystery but simply a manifest truth. We know Him through His creations, through His signs, through His manifestations. Once we know Him, we will be inclined to praise Him, worship Him, and to submit to Him. We only submit to Him to be good, to do good, to think right, and to act fairly and justly. The way a worker earns wages for his or her work, God similarly rewards good deeds. While the reward of human beings is limited, God's reward is unlimited and timeless. His reward for us is to enjoy happiness forever. Thus, we can perpetuate our happiness, beyond time and worldly enjoyment. That is a real victory, a victory that involves no loss, damages, or miseries. Knowledge about God is indispensable because it is in light of God that every creation makes sense and the unknown and unidentified come to be known. Without knowledge of God, one seems to be an orphan who does not know his or her parents, a traveler who is lost, a seeker who cannot find whatever has been aimed for, a toiler whose struggles avail nothing, a sower who reaps little, an expectant whose expectation falls flat, an aspirant whose aspiration fails, a crusader whose crusades lead up to nowhere. Objection may arise that all seekers may have attained their purpose, that the toilers have been paid off, that the sowers have reaped their fruits, that the aspirants have reached their aspirations and the crusaders have succeeded. Perhaps in the short run, perhaps under the cloak of time, which is a partition between life and death.

To conclude, the knowledge of God is the most valuable, most indispensable gift leading towards perpetual happiness, and no other knowledge will be as effective and productive as this. In fact, this is the only knowledge that gives meaning to all other knowledge, encompasses all information and experiences, unravels many secrets, makes us feel comfortable about uncertainties, and inspires us to be hopeful and positive. That is why it is called the heart of knowledge, the mother of all other knowledge. In the same way that heart is indispensable for life, knowledge of God is indispensable for our happiness.

7

WISDOM VERSUS INTELLECT

Although *wisdom* and *intellect* are used interchangeably in our daily writing and conversation, in essence, they are distinct from each other in certain ways, each one being endowed with its own denomination and description. Wisdom could be divinely inspired, or it may come from a very insightful person; therefore, its validity excels that of intellect, which proceeds from anyone who is capable of thinking.

If you know about the wisdom of King Solomon and Loqman the Sagacious, they were both enjoying divine wisdom. One of the stories of Solomon has come to us as follows: Two women, in company with a child, came to Solomon contentiously. They were accusing each other of child theft, and each one was trying to convince King Solomon of being the child's real mother. Solomon asked for a sword, announcing his decree to the women, ordering to cut the living child in two and give half to one woman and half to the other. The woman, who was the child's real mother, was deeply moved out of love and said to the king: "Give her the living baby? Don't kill him!" The king discovered the real mother and gave the child to her.

The following things draw a distinction between *wisdom* and *intellect*: One, wisdom can be a divine inspiration. Two, wisdom comes from the truthful, spiritual, and sagacious people. Three, wisdom always leads to truth, not necessarily the intellect. Four, wisdom can be convincing from

25

the beginning to the end, while the intellect may convince at the outset, but its outcome could be contradictory. Five, wisdom always comes to be accurate, but the intellect may lie, mislead, harm, or be abused. Six, wisdom belongs to a few, but intellect to anyone who can think. And thus, wisdom gets the better of intellect.

8

CAN EDUCATION STAND TODAY'S TRIALS?

Education, contributing to all aspects of humanity, is apt to be the most important dimension of every single society. As a prophet, it should teach ethics and morality; as a leader, it should seek people's peace, prosperity, and freedom; as an educator, it should teach people how to build their intellect and character; how to learn skills, values, and manners; how to enhance other most important merits and characteristics; and how to contribute to economy, social needs, creativity, and productivity. To use the power of education as a solution will not bring about overnight results; however, proper use of education will induce striking changes as time goes by.

Education is thought to be always and everywhere positive and bright, and it seems absurd to think of it as a system of corruption. Actually, sometimes education has been used by interest groups as a weapon of abuse. Such abuses have occurred in multiple forms and different times politically, socially, educationally, historically, and psychologically. Education has been used by individuals or groups to support a certain ideology to keep their interests intact. It has been used to brainwash the people, to persuade them to achieve a certain goal, to propagandize, and to influence. Corruption in education is more dangerous because it could be disguised in a beautiful form that it is hard, or needs a lot of discretion, to ascertain its true nature and disbelieve or deny it. To display this danger, for example, a corrupt educated person will be far worse than a corrupt uneducated person, as Theodore Roosevelt says, "A man who has never gone to school may steal from a freight car; but if he has a university education, he may steal the whole railroad." This is also true of the 2008 financial crisis, which was the product of highly educated minds.

To flunk students to improve them is a negative idea; to flunk them out of colleges is even a subversive idea. They feel despaired and down to fail. Unless utterly unprepared to learn, students must succeed; therefore, failure reflects more negligence of the instructors rather than that of the students. There are learning strategies even for unprepared students. Exertion will lead to success. Fairness, objectivity, and understanding are the marks of good educators, besides mastery of their curriculum.

The mission of education to moralize and edify has become a great deal complicated due to the changes and developments that have happened in the course of time. In fact, as our generation has been getting smarter and smarter, the humanity's fate has been subject to further trials; therefore, it is incumbent upon our education to get wiser and wiser

Today's technological progress has been enchanting, and the pleasure and comfort of life have been intriguing. Having put our full trust upon technology and its ever-increasing advancement, we are expecting the best out of it, as if in good hands. Although in good hands, we have undermined our inner world: internal harmony—an equilibrium between emotional, cognitive, and volition---which is vital for our well-being. As the time has rolled by and means and instruments of comfort have augmented, fraud and corruption have multiplied. This correlation has given rise to an important aspect having taken shape alongside passage of time: character degeneration, which is a form of spiritual sickness. Spiritual sickness cannot be seen the way physical illness is spotted, because the former is invisible, the latter visible. Even so, only a prudent mind can discover such degeneration. In fact, spiritual degeneration surfaces indirectly through other phenomena. That is, the more spiritual degeneration comes to pass, the more evil things such as evil acts, evil feelings, and evil thoughts proliferate. Theodore Roosevelt prescribes the significance of morality in education: "To educate a man in mind and not in morals is to educate a menace to society."

Technologically, all kinds of facilities are available to live comfortably. In fact, people are not suffering from lack of technical resources, nor are they in need of discovering more and inventing more to create more comfort. They need an education emphasizing spiritual and ethical values to create the kind of character needed to consider human values and goodness, focusing on common human needs, and seeking sensible ways of solving human problems. People suffer from the way these resources are accessed, distributed, used, and manipulated; the way human resources and abilities are spent, or the way they are left unused or misused, etc. It is ideal to aspire to further opportunities to build better relationship, to sow seed of trust to rely on each other without reservation and suspicion, to inspire and promote moral and ethical values, to establish and develop spiritual values, to leave behind all kinds of prejudice and partiality, to provide ideas and resources and possibilities to promote sense of cooperation between individuals, to teach responsibly and properly, to discover the ability and creativity of the students and furbish them, to have a complete awareness of social, economical, moral, educational, political, and psychological needs, and try to meet them,. These and many other things should be attended to and handled properly. There are important human needs that will be served by free human qualities and attributes such as goodwill, efforts, honesty, patience, conscience, good heart, sense of cooperation, and other mental and spiritual assets benefiting us a great deal aside from material resources.

Given what is said, today's prospective education not only should prepare people for jobs, careers, and opportunities to achieve economic goals, but also accomplish moral and ethical achievements. If this is put into practice, education will be the most important harbinger of a win-win situation. And thus becoming a champion, it will be led towards Solomonic wisdom, spreading its blessing, it will change, inspire, and enlighten even those who are street-smarts.

Today's education motto should be epitomized as truth, integrity, cooperation, inspiration, and liberation. Education should promote abilities and skills to distinguish between right and wrong, so that we abandon what is wrong and follow what is right, no matter be it spiritual, social, political, economical, or intellectual, as far as it nourishes true feelings. Education should encourage those values that are worthy and beautiful, and, as a most credible weapon, liberate humanity from all bonds and conditions that prevent their growth mentally, physically, emotionally, and spiritually.

It should open up people's mind to discover their true nature, to improve their shortcomings, to cultivate good relationship between individuals, to make them acquainted with their responsibilities, to evaluate their performance fairly, to give them opportunities to use their abilities, to nourish their faculties, to learn new skills, to utilize human resources appropriately, and to find ways to use those resources having been left unused.

Education should open a new chapter to prepare leaders for leadership; of course, all types and ranks of leaderships, from family to political, to clerical, to financial, and to all other kinds of leaderships. Emphasis on creating sound leadership must be a crucial priority of education. The question that who should create such a standard to be modeled on by the leaders is apt to be a totality of experiences, knowledge, trials and errors that have been the legacy of centuries old. This is a tremendous experience that has been collected by international leaders during the course of history covering a myriad of historical, political, social, spiritual, intellectual, and educational experiences, including all ranks and strata.

Educators as educational leaders are bound to create the most comfortable atmosphere for teaching. Educators should be fully capable not only of whatever they teach but also be conscientious of fulfilling their job in the best possible way. Educators' mastery of the subject is crucial, so is crucial to prepare the right teaching environment. The right environment is an important part of teaching. It is through this strategy that the students are inspired to learn and to participate for learning. This strategy consists of multiple teaching phenomena such as psychological, educational, intellectual, and behavioral perspectives. The educator must have the right behavior for teaching. Sacrifices, perseverance, patience, sense of humor, affection, tolerance, and understanding are some of the characteristics that an educator should have. Given all this, the best learning environment will be created, and the students will interact. An educator should be a hallmark of truth, humanity, and cooperation. It should be a common truth for an educator to distinguish between right and wrong, good and bad. Arrogance, ostentatiousness, bragging, contempt, intolerance, and prejudice are some of the egregious characteristics that damage the wholesomeness of personality, proving to be the stigmas of humanity. An educator should identify them, get rid of them, and warn others against them. One of the effective teaching schemes is that the more the potential of a student be discovered and utilized, the more the teaching takes effect. Potential of the students should be fully used and discovered.

Affordability of college is another important aspect to be considered. Education should be available for all, and all barriers should be averted. Educational institutions should be morally oriented, not commercially. As long as the people depend on college, they should also be assured of its return. Let education define and specify the prejudice, and not vice versa. Let education solve not only our present dilemmas but also lead us into the future that is safe and promising.

Can education stand today's trials? The answer will be positive only to the extent the above ideals—truth, integrity, cooperation, inspiration, and liberation—be assimilated into education and exercised.

9

BEAUTY

Beauty, despite most other universals, is multidimensional. Physically, it encapsulates features involving many characters and characteristics that stimulate complex human sentiments and sensations, inspiring a good amount of appreciation and adoration. Various physical features fuel different sentiments: Perhaps a beautiful woman creates sensational feelings; natural scenes such as a starry night, a northern pole aurora, a sunset or sunrise, a garden of flowers or fruit, may trigger appreciative feelings; however, a beautiful house, car, or painting may give rise to an enthusiastic sentiment galvanizing craving and allure.

Cognitively, beauty involves intellectual manifestations that bring about admiration. A beautiful idea, intention, or purpose, creates appreciation. Ideas, intentions, and plans are not all beautiful. They could be destructive, miserable, and dark.

Literally, beauty is manifested in literary works such as poetry, drama, novel, proverb, etc. Authors of literary works could have all the means, ways, and methods to manifest beauty universally. Emotionally, beauty becomes a manifestation of grandest qualities such as love, compassion, joy, trust, friendship, etc. The way these qualities are cherished, so are their beauty.

Beauty is a great deal accompanied by artistic phenomena including literary, sculptural, musical, theatrical, painting, etc. All the talent, work, and artistry of human beings are part of this beauty.

Spiritually, beauty is portrayed in its purest, holiest, and most sublime form, encompassing emotional, literal, and cognitive features. What is worthy, what is sublime, what is noble, and what is inspiring are actually gifted and accompanied with the delight of spiritual beauty. Spiritual accomplishment is the most beautiful of all because of its purity, longevity, and nobility.

Beauty could be one of the strongest and most proven signs of divine creation. Beauty has been contributed to all dimensions of creation, visible or invisible. Symmetry or harmony is an elemental phenomenon of beauty. People who have less or no understanding of beauty, turn their God-given symmetrical dimension into insensible and raw caricature by leaving their hair or beard grow as wild as weeds, or by donning repugnant clothing. They are the ones who adulterate the creation and remain ignorant to what God has bestowed on them. Hair and beard and ugly clothes will give them no credits of any kind, neither in this world nor in the afterworld.

10

OF GOOD AND EVIL

Good and evil have been discussed repeatedly, interpreted differently, viewed from various perspectives, and have been the cynosure of discussion of both ordinary and elite people across the history of mankind. As far as people were cognizant of the dark and light, so were they familiar with good and evil. As a matter of fact, darkness was viewed as a negative thing, having been a threat and trepidation to the people. Good has been viewed as a source of light and happiness.

Good and evil, the most polemical and controversial concepts, are commonplace terms used repeatedly in our daily verbal and written language, and their examples are shown in various thoughts, actions, behaviors, and our daily affairs.

To define evil in terms of standing, it is a miasma of despair and bitterness. It is infamous, whose notoriety is displayed and felt as much in the same way as buildings are burned to the ground, people are murdered, women are raped, crimes are committed, robberies are perpetrated, and all other enormities are performed. To define evil as an entity, it is overwhelming in terms of nastiness, poverty, and horror. It engenders corruption enormously but nefariously. Anywhere it goes, it pollutes. Anywhere it stays, it contaminates. Whatever it performs, it fouls and brings blight. It eats poison, and it spawns plague…. As an artist, it is so wily that all it does is depravation and sin; however, despite its all enormity, it is such an attraction that its fans are increasing every moment, and they are ignoring its crimes as if they are spellbound or absentminded of its consequences. Its attraction resembles that of pyrethrums killing their victims, or that of sirens luring unwary sailors onto rocks. It is already in extreme despair straits, and the more evil is added, its desperation augmented. Evil has many signs and sources to be cognizant of: a bad action, an ugly behavior, a corrupt decision, a conspiracy, and all obnoxious plans are of such examples. There are a myriad of examples for each one of those categories that account for evil phenomena, and each single individual can commit as many atrocities as possible, performing as many obnoxious behaviors as possible.

Etymologically, good and evil have been used as adjectives and nouns, and sometimes informally as an adverb. As an adjective, good means fine, excellent, virtuous, obedient, well-behaved, right, proper, capable, close and intimate, healthy, pleasant, kind, convenient, safe to eat, valuable, clear and sunny, etc. As a noun, it signifies virtue, goodness, honesty, truth, purity, etc. As an adverb, it is used informally as healthy and in a good mood. For example, I feel good, but *I feel well* means I am healthy.

Evil as an adjective means bad, wrong, immoral, sinful, corrupt dark, despicable, etc. As a noun, it denotes badness, sin, immorality, hardship, misery, affliction, etc.

In literature, good and evil have been used a great deal explicitly, implicitly, metaphorically, and similarly. Good has usually presented sound, sophisticated, positive character and characteristic; evil has portrayed ugly, unfair, cruel, and stupid characters. Conflicts and inconsistencies portray forces of evil and good in literature. These conflicts could be human vs. himself or herself, human vs. nature, human vs. human, human vs. the Devil, etc. In Oscar Wilde's *Dorian Gray,* the conflict happens between Dorian and society on the one hand, and between Dorian and himself on the other. In Christopher Marlowe's *Dr. Faustus,* the conflict surfaces between good and evil. Dr. Faustus, though highly educated and intelligent, relinquishes his soul to the devil in exchange for power and knowledge. In Shakespeare's *Hamlet,* the conflict happens between Hamlet and his uncle Claudius. In *Cinderella,* beauty stands for good, ugliness for evil. In Shakespeare's *Macbeth,* good and evil live together inside Macbeth. Evil defeats good when Macbeth murders the king. Good defeats evil when Macbeth is slain. As we notice, all these conflicts transpire between good and evil. In the same way, this is also true of the Greek and Roman imaginary gods who are either in conflict with themselves or with human beings for different causes to avenge each other in some way.

The main question about good and evil arises to ask whether they are real or just unreal, nominal, or symbolic. As it was mentioned, good and evil are used both symbolically as common nouns and realistically as proper nouns. For example, when we are saying sin, oppression, robbery, rape, murder, etc. are evil or acts of evil, we are making use of symbolism, similes, or metaphors. The same is true of goodness, justice, truth, virtue, integrity, decency, etc. But once we are using good and evil subjectively, then their presence becomes real and convincing. It is then that God stands for good and the Devil or the Evil One stands for evilness or evil. Of course, the expression of the Devil taking stand against the transgressors make sense, but the Devil versus God is absurd and false, because one is the Creator, the other the creature; one is all mighty, all knowing, all seeing, all hearing, the other cursed, ignorant, and fallen. Therefore, to get into a showdown with God is stupid.

In fact, evil is as real as transgressions like murder, rape, robbery, tyranny, fraud, etc. As far as those misdeeds exist, so does evil. As about the reality of God, He is so universal, so manifest that His manifestation spreads from micro to macro. And it is again the work of the Devil who deludes those people whose eyes and minds have been screened from the sight of such manifestation

To define and introduce good and evil in terms of theological and divine account is very crucial. The moment of truth arrived when God created man to put the Devil to test, and he failed it. In fact, Lucifer (known as the Satan, the Devil, the Evil One, or Iblis), who was enjoying the angelic kingdom among the angels, lost the trial of God by rejecting His command: He did not deign to prostrate before Adam. Once he disobeyed, God cursed him and expelled him from the heaven. Thus, Lucifer turns into evil, vowing to take his revenge from humanity by attacking them mentally and emotionally. Therefore, evil stands for wickedness, misery, sin, badness, villainy, and dishonesty. In this context, good stands for goodness, truth, honesty, etc. As a matter of fact, good the absolute stands for God, and evil stands for the Devil. Writers usually have put one above the other. For example, in many cases, a bad character or characteristic has prevailed against the good one or vice versa. However, in reality, good has been considered a light, evil darkness. In fact, light overwhelms darkness, not the other way round. Of course, to compare the power of the Devil with that of humans is of no consequence. One may triumph over the other, depending upon the human qualities and personality. As about comparing the power of the Devil with God results from ignorance. Such comparison will be true of those who have no idea about the Creator in the first place, or those who misestimate Him in the second place.

When we are left undefended and vulnerable, Evil not only overwhelms us like darkness and attacks us like miseries, but it also confines us like a prison. He will mentally and spiritually defeat us, making us completely deluded, so that we will be at our wits' end, and by committing crimes and breaking the established norms, we are sent into the jails, our hands cuffed, our feet chained.

It is ironic that we do not know we are confined by the evil, in the first place, and that being in prison in real life has been the cause of the Devil's conspiracies, in the second place. As a matter of fact, we are spiritually imprisoned when we have sinned. We lose our freedom by becoming a servant of the Devil. We give the rein of our life to him and he drags us anywhere he wants. Once we are his servants, we become a servant of our desire, our passion, our greed, our pride, our ambitions, etc. We become a servant of greed, for example, by hoarding up wealth illegally, unconscientiously, and immorally.

There are certain abilities and desires in human beings to which the Evil One appeals and thereby enslaves us. For example, our pride provokes us to aspire to ambitions even at times at the cost of trespassing fairness. We lust to possess power to gallop the horse of desire, no matter how evil it is.

Love of money leads to greed and unfairness. Self-indulgence in eating and having sex is another evil that leads to enormous miseries and health dilemmas. Freedom is another phenomenon that has been mostly abused and therefore has unleashed catastrophic impacts.

To be sure, it is not viable to defeat the Devil without the help of Providence. Therefore, the more we are away from the care and protection of God, the closer we are to the grasp of the Devil. Although the Devil has no advantage to attack or affect us physically, he does have an upper hand to attack us mentally and emotionally. Have you thought how Eve was deceived into eating the forbidden fruit? Have you thought about how Cain was persuaded to kill his brother Able? Have you thought how Abraham could not convince his father to accept his religion? Have you thought about how Noah failed to convince his son to board the ship? All this has happened through the conspiracies of the Devil.

Thus, all the transgressions are inspired by the Devil. There is not even a single sin that has not been shared or supported by the Devil. In fact, he has a share in all crimes committed by the humanity: homicides, rapes, robberies, assaults, hate crimes, arsons, briberies, batteries, child abuse, child pornography, conspiracies, misbehaviors, disturbing the peace, burglaries, distortions, forgeries, frauds, kidnapping, prostitutions, sexual assaults, etc.

This does not mean that we can dodge accountabilities for these transgressions. In fact, we have not been forced into these transgressions to find an excuse to stop shouldering those responsibilities. We have been induced and seduced into them, in which there is no indication of compulsion. As long as we are free committing things, we are responsible for them, and we will pay for our wrong

11

THE TWO WORLDS

The macrocosm and microcosm—whole and part or human being and the universe—is a blend of each other. However, human beings prove their immortality by being endowed with soul, on the one hand, and substantiating their difference from the universe by enjoying volitional, emotive, and cognitive phenomena, on the other.

We are always dealing with two worlds, living in them, and experiencing them. One is inside us, the other outside. Our internal world is established within ourselves with the woof and weft of our own entities; however, it is capable of getting out of its own niche, going beyond its sovereignty, connecting to and sharing with the outside world. Our internal world is made of physical, mental, emotional, and volitional phenomena. External world is made of matter.

The two worlds are in immediate contact with each other, as if there is a door between them wherewith all connections are established and all information is exchanged.

The external world is as complex, diverse, subtle, profuse, and ingenuous as our internal world. There are truths about them that we have not yet discovered, things that we have not yet seen, boundaries that are beyond our reach, facts that we have not ascertained, information that has been left undetected and latent.

41

Both of them are controlled by laws, fortified by reason, and designed elaborately.

These two worlds have been made of both esoteric and exoteric phenomena. Each one assumes its complexity in its own way. External world is enjoying vast extension of space-time, which, as far as it is visible, is entirely material. However, the external world complexity will increase when it falls beyond the reach of our understanding. Although the external world is made of matter, there are physical substances endowed with their own nature and properties, each one distinct from the other. For example, carbyne is an allotrope of carbon, which is 40 times stiffer than diamond, and it is single dimensional. There might be such more elements, even with more exotic specifications that we know nothing about, or, In the same way, as there are varieties in living objects such as plants and animals, so is in inanimate objects such as elements, compounds, mixtures, or any other fields of matter. There are elements or objects that are not yet discovered. The reason they have left undiscovered is because either they are unknown to us, for they have escaped our observation, or because they are too distant from us to perceive them, such as dark matter, whereof we are just theorizing. By what is said, what is happening within a human proves to be more intricate and delicate than what is going on without. For example, the internal world, besides mental and emotional phenomena, is dealing with the sovereignty of the soul, which has nothing to do with the external world and is indifferent towards matter. As a matter of fact, we need it, not it us, just like shoes or clothes that we need, not they us.

Our body, which is made of material phenomena, is living along with the external world. Heart, among all other human organs and biological systems, though made of physical entity, which is prone to decay and aging, is a great source of emotions such as love, compassion, regret, grief, happiness, etc. Therefore, the heart could influence the soul by means of both its benevolence and malevolence. For instance, charitable emotion brings goodness; malignant emotion induces evilness, leading to unfavorable consequences. In the aftermath of these impacts, the human soul is either being nourished, enjoying great expansion, or it is neglected and suppressed, so that its growth is greatly affected.

Thus, our brain and heart, which are made of matter, are capable of serving the purpose both internally and externally. When sharing love and compassion with others, they interact with the external world, and like other decomposable organic matter, they age and decay. When they are occupied with deliberation and thoughts, for instance, devoting themselves to loving and caring of universals such as beauty, truth, and goodness, they purpose internally.

Our mental and emotional phenomena can live within their own world independently. However, their connection with the external world gives them perfection, growth, and extra dimensions. The more we associate with external resources, the more we increase our experience, and the more we learn. Our mind and heart are open to multiple opportunities and avenues to learn, to discover, and to grow. In the same way that we learn from external phenomena and experiences, we are also improving our thoughts and emotions by taking advantage of internal phenomena and experiences. Once we have collected information from the external world, we can use it internally for our growth by digesting, evaluating, and pondering it.

Our senses are open to the external world like windows: our sight catches a glimpse of shapes, motions, colors, dimensions, objects, lines, sizes, and other details. Our sense of hearing detects all the sound waves, facilitating communication. Our sense of smell detects all the odors. Our sense of touch detects all the sensations such as cold, hot, smooth, rough, itch, pain, vibration, tickle, etc. Our sense of taste helps us discover all kinds of tastes such as sweetness, bitterness, saltiness, sourness, and deliciousness. Thus, these human senses function like windows opening to information as means of interactions between external and internal worlds.

What is worthy of mentioning is that our understanding outlook is not reduced only to what we get through these senses. Although they open our mental outlook, change our knowledge, and expand our understanding, they cannot define our inner self, intuitive understanding and insight. This portion of perception is the totality of experiences that go beyond the boundary of senses, a dimension that divides worldly experiences from spiritual experiences. In fact, worldly experiences may suggest spiritual significance, especially for those who are open-minded. What makes our inner world worthy and special is its spiritual significance, which appears to be a rare light connecting us to eternity, and gives us indirect intimations to comprehend it, if we deserve it and are prepared for it. It also acquaints us with subtle and invisible phenomena such as soul, spirit, and demonic world. Most important of all, it enlightens us about God, establishing connections between the known and unknown, and leading us to esoteric experiences. It also deals with intricate mental, psychological, and spiritual spheres, helping us to explain delicate experiences.

Humans possess very complex entities, whose intricacies are much more than those of the external world. For example, the external world entirely reduces to matter and nothing more than the matter, which everything comes under a single entity; that is, material entity. When we come to human life, it extends to multiple entities. In the first place, it divides into material and immaterial entities. Its material entities including organs, systems, and other parts made of living cells, our basic building blocks. In the second place, an immaterial entity extends to other multiple entities such as mental, spiritual, emotional, volitional, etc.

In fact, cells are the basic building blocks for organisms; atoms are the basic building blocks for matter. Although these building blocks both matter, it makes a huge difference the way they are laid out, and the purpose they are serving.

Humans, whose body is apparently made of the same atoms and molecules as everything else, are mind-bogglingly far more complex, full of wonders and fascination, and mind-blowing. This complexity underlies a good number of things including complexity of physiological structures of organs, organ systems, human cells, and other human parts. Each one of these organs or organ systems is so complex that it is like a marvelous independent machine; however, they work in perfect unison indefatigably, unfailingly. For example, certain parts of humans such as the heart and brain are enjoying not only material property but also spiritual property; for example, the heart is not only a piece of flesh but also a source of emotions harboring love, sympathy, friendship, joy, anticipation, trust, sadness, etc. Similarly, the brain, in association with supernatural phenomena, is open to such divine, insightful, profound, and esoteric information that ordinary matter cannot apprehend.

Further, humans are gifted with cognitive, emotional, and volitional phenomena, which epitomize not only complexity but also prove to be astonishingly awe-inspiring.

Another important phenomenon that brings distinction between human and the universe is *freedom*, which the former enjoys, not the latter. That is why, humans are blessed with creativity to create and discover, blessed with intellect to think and recognize, blessed with freedom to act and perform of their own volition, to gain or lose, to be a devil or an angel, to be a sage or an ignorant, to be full or empty. In fact, the material universe is incapable of all this.

12

PAIN VERSUS PLEASURE

If this question were posed: Does pleasure make sense? It will be laughed off because it is deemed inconceivable to challenge something that has been thought to be the sweets of life. And now this question: Does suffering make sense? It will prick the mind to check it out.

When you come into the world, you bring pain, and when you leave the world, you feel the pain. Given all this, do you see any mysteries in pain?

Now this question: How have the following glorious men—who have had no intention but serving humanity, establishing the truth, saving the souls, and enlightening the peoples, and whose gain has been nothing else but Gods' pleasure—given sacrifices and suffered throughout their lives inconsequentially?

Adam and Eve were thrown out of paradise and embroiled in a life full of hardship and miseries. Noah was ridiculed and insulted by the people. Prophet Joseph suffered years of adversities and imprisonment and hardship. Prophet Moses wandered 40 years in the desert, spending a life full of affliction, tribulations, and challenges. Prophet Jesus encountered many atrocities and challenges. Prophet Mohammad similarly suffered from conflicts, numerous despicable reactions of the people, barbaric behaviors, and such many other dilemmas. In fact, these models of humanity sacrificed enormously for the happiness and prosperity of the people, but they themselves lived in abject poverty and hardship, without expecting anything from anyone. In the face of all this, do you find any reason or mystery to justify their suffering and affliction? Or do you think their suffering has been of no avail?

Pleasure and pain are two greatest ingredients of life. They are so familiar, so universal, and so ubiquitous that people believe they know enough about them, and therefore they do not need to dig into them any further. This way of thinking has been a good cause for pleasure and pain to remain undiscovered and opaque, just like those individuals who have been alienated from their sweet selves, and, to their regret, having always been blind to this realization. As a matter of fact, these two phenomena, which are universally known, are hiding the most precious secrets of life.

As a matter of fact, the law of pleasure is different from the law of pain. Pleasure never wants to be in the same state. Like a balloon, it always tends to dilate; like a tree, it grows; like an epidemic, it spreads out; like a gaseous volcano, it heightens; like a storm, it gains momentum, but it is loath to diminish, to attenuate, to reduce, to fade, and to devitalize. Pleasure goes along with severity, pitilessness, arrogance, madness, violence, passion, excitement, tantrum, rashness, resentment, envy, and lasciviousness. That is why it may lead to vice, to negative changes.

Suffering is inevitable, to our regret. We suffer and inflict suffering from the time we are born to the time when we die. Suffering is a universal phenomenon, from which nobody is safe, even the one who claims to be the happiest one on earth. Suffering is inflicted bodily, emotionally, and psychologically.

There are many forms of suffering, such as pain and injury, torture, disease, violence, grief, depression, anxiety, etc.

On the contrary, pleasure is always sought further and further, and a pleasant future is expected and wished for fervently. Happy feelings increase the heart pulsation, creating excitement, desires flourishing and exhilarating, wishes augmenting, and when pleasurable, the time flies quickly. Suffering may affect the heart, drying up our desire, killing our excitement, and slowing down time.

Pleasure and pain have different directions and different agenda. Pleasure tends to move centripetally, pain centrifugally; that is, the former tends to move towards the center, the latter away from the center. The more the pleasurers enjoy their lives, the more they tend to move towards the centripetal force, while the sufferers tend to move towards centrifugal force. In the former instance, they become self-centered and self-absorbed; in the latter instance, they tend to move away from themselves and seek other people's support and love. This is why those who suffer look for others to pour out their pain to them to lighten their burden from their shoulders. But the pleasurers love to brag about their triumph and success to others.

Pleasure has a limited dimension, definite meaning, and predictable outcome, perhaps with little subtlety. Suffering enjoys much deeper meaning, extensive subtlety, substantial mysteries, and hidden outcomes. Pleasure belongs more to the present rather than to the future; suffering belongs more to the future rather than to the present. Suffering comes most of the time without knowledge abruptly from the blue: we lose someone; we lose something; we feel ill; we are afflicted by a disaster; we feel depressed; we are tortured; we are intimidated;

our desires are not met; etc. Sometimes pain seizes us so tremendously that we mentally and physically become transfixed. Suffering we cannot avoid though we wish to. It is thrust upon us suddenly, and we cannot help but accept this inhospitable guest immediately. However, I want to underscore that suffering is deeper, subtler, and more suggestive than joy. Pleasure is a transitory feeling whose impression is limited and local, despite the suffering whose impression goes beyond, and it is associated with meaning and ramification.

Sources of suffering are as many as sources of happiness, perhaps more than the sources of happiness. It could come anytime from anywhere, anyone, and anything. Sometimes suffering comes from within, other times from without; from within, in the form of depression, hopelessness, disease, or bodily decadence, etc. From outside, it comes either from other human beings in the form of war, animosity, competition, conflicts, rejection, abandoning, rape, robbing, jealousy, greed, deception, hate, contempt, birth, death, old age, murder, failure, loss, bodily injuries and pain, defeat, and frustration. There is one more kind of suffering that comes from the external world, a source that is beyond human control, such as famine, earthquake, epidemics, and other disasters

While pleasure goes with excitement, pride, hope, high expectations, and desires, Pain usually consorts with compassion, impotence, reluctance, inaction, and lack of vigor. Pain sometimes leads to great changes. It is generally desired to have it on the wane, vanquished. Sometimes pain leads to positive changes. I know those who have experienced excruciating pain in their chests for having heart attacks have changed their diets and lifestyles. Thus, painful experiences lead to great changes, growth, and extraordinary lessons. For example, Diana Nyad, who broke records as a long-distance swimmer, swam from Cuba to Florida, in 1979, breaking a 30-year record, braving jellyfish stings, shark attacks, wild waves, storms, and other dangers. Her painful experiences taught her great lessons.

On certain occasions, suffering takes us to the past, causing us to reflect upon our experiences and to make sense of our suffering, so that we look for restitution of what has been done in the past. Other times, it takes us to the future to learn something new— new experiences, new feelings, or a different quest. Thus, suffering people get acquainted with new situations, whereof they learn fresh lessons and get used to new conditions. That is like living in a new world, facing the changes. Thus, people not only entertain changes in their own lives, but they also feel other people who are suffering, a feeling that makes them closer to the sufferers. Sara Teresa Shafer introduces suffering as 'the great equalizer: a figurative connective tissue that binds human beings to each other psychically and physically.'

On the aesthetic level, suffering has navigated a far-reaching sphere. As a representation form, suffering has effectively been translated into the arts. Poets, dramatists, novelists, and other artists have incorporated various forms of suffering in their works to meet different purposes and explain various ideas. Both Plato and Aristotle argue that tragic dramas accord catharsis or purgation to the audience to purify their emotion. The purgation takes place when the audience is moved to pity and fear by a tragic character. The audience feel pity when they are acquainted with the character's tragedy, and they feel fear when they put themselves in the character's shoes, experiencing the tragic situation, and feeling the danger of misdeed. Characters suffer from different causes: Hamlet suffers because of his deceptive uncle; Ophelia because of her failed love; Dante Rossetti suffers because of his beloved Lizzie Siddal's death, his poems nestled in her coffin to show his love and cherish her love posthumously; so does Othello because of his poor judgment; so does Orual, C. S. Lewis's character in *Till We Have Faces*; same is true of Oscar Wild's Picture of Dorian Gray as a result of internal pain and conflict. In fact, there is a tremendous amount of literature, art, and thoughts about war and its impact. Truly, war has been the most damaging source of suffering.

The more we understand the nature of pleasure, the more we discover our strength and weakness against it and avail ourselves of it properly. As human beings are a composite of bodily, mental, and spiritual elements, most of the time there are dissensions and conflicts between those phenomena. This conflict is created mostly by sensual desires thirsty for pleasure, which gives rise to greed, pride, and ambition—a threat to the integrity, wholeness, and intactness of human beings. Desires are the springboard of emotion. Love, passion, and joy, with ecstasy marking its peak, are components of emotion, and they are teeming with pleasure. They express intimate sentiments and relationships both divine and somatic. Love plays a major role. Getting excited by pleasure, emotion may turn into violence if it is given free rein. Passion, strong and hardly controllable emotion, at times makes incursions against cognitive and spiritual phenomena, disturbing the peace of mind, ravaging the integrity of soul. Given this situation, pleasure is wreaking havoc. Many a time, passion and lust disguise themselves as love, tearing apart harmony and peace.

As the pleasurers are in immediate contact with pleasure, their senses are all inundated with it, so that they think of or care for nothing but epicurean feasts and sensual gratification, whose lives dazzle with sensuality, and whose mental and spiritual power is crushed under the servitude of worldly desires. They sacrifice their time and efforts for those things that satisfy their taste and desire; for example, sensational desire becomes acute in them, so does gluttony. These two agents become so demanding that they overshadow most other activities and aspects, their lives becoming a handful of sensations. Thus, sensual gratification is deemed to be their most ideal business. They think this is the right way to serve themselves, and they think they serve themselves in a perfect way. In fact, by doing so, they are doing themselves s disservice, because they become so estranged with themselves that they lose their real identity.

While through pleasure we become alienated from our true self, through suffering we could find our way to our original intactness, or at least we will come to realize how much we have lost our integrity and wholesomeness. Once we explore our disintegrated self, then we will take care of it and try to put it back aright.

A pleasurable life is teeming with desires, opportunities, and much hustles and bustles. Desires are open to multiple ways, and each way is opening to further pleasure and gratification. A life crowded with desires is moved with greed, a point where gratification is not easy to be fulfilled. At this point, the pleasurers are getting drowned in their desire, as if they are given to intoxication. They think they are in a perfect state of mind because they enjoy themselves. Thus, they nourish their bestial desires by abandoning their common sense, attending to their bodily needs, and leaving their spiritual world in abject deprivation.

And finally, this question: Do you think exhilaration, which energizes the heart, should be considered a blessing, but depression, which affects the heart, a token of misfortune? Of course, the disparity is striking. Who knows? I am confident that God does pay attention to the cry of an orphan, to the suffering of needy people, and to the pain of the sick. Suffering has meaning and gravity. It is not a footstep impression to be wiped out from the ground, or a wave to be lost in the midst of the ocean, or a wind to be lost among the trees. There is a reason behind each suffering. John O'Donohue, Irish priest, poet, and philosopher says, 'One of the best teachers in the world is suffering.' Nietzsche was seeking health through sickness. E. Cassel argues, 'After the experience of suffering, the person is led to a richer understanding of the meaning of being human, a greater concern for suffering of others, and away from the superficialities that too often characterize daily existence.' If we think of happiness as an end, suffering is definitely a means to an end. Perhaps the disadvantaged will be entitled to a better share. In fact, pleasure is appreciated when suffering is felt.

13

NUDE OR ARTISTIC?

Recently, "Reclining Nude," a painting by Amedeo Modigliani, was sold for $179.4 million at Christie's auction in Manhattan to a Chinese collector. The painting portrays a nude woman reclining on a red couch, blue cushion. I wonder if this deal was the effect of tableau's artistic success or its nude and sensational effect.

I highly value works of art, and they deserve to sell valuably. Thus, I feel no grudge or envy if I make mention of the exorbitant price of the above-mentioned piece of art. However, I allow myself to confess that most of the time sensation gains the upper hand over the reason. Sensation not only pumps our desire in art but in a variety of other fields and walks of life. Different sensations bring about different results. Sensation works better and quicker because it overshadows the mind, grasps the helm of life in its hand, and runs the boat of life wherever and whenever it wants. It makes the stunts to risk their lives by performing extraordinary activities to achieve fame and honor. It turns the money makers into greedy folks, inducing the power seekers to commit all unimaginable things to be the toast of power and recognition, inspiring the fanatics with subversive innovations and religiosity, galvanizing the zealots to abuse their dire sentiments for personal interests, persuading a group of people who deem to be distinct and pure-blooded to stay high above others, inciting a number of people to be arrogant and self-important. Thus, it has also persuaded the Chinese buyer to pay such an extravagant amount for "Reclining Nude."

What sensational success is hidden in the tableau? Nudity, artistic success, or other efficacies? Perhaps a blend of all this, but the effectiveness and psychological perspective of auction and marketing is the most effective of all. Several causes come together at the auction to excite the bidders to lift the price of an item to the roof. Sensation is the special potion whereby the entire audience is intoxicated with. In addition to sensation, there are a number of other roles that are dominant there, such as the role of recognition, honor, and fame; the role of power; the role of egotism and arrogance. In fact, in this gathering, the bidders are set against one another to compete with each other in purchasing the item. When a product is presented, one makes a bid, which is followed by the second, the third, and so on, so that the more the bidders are added the price goes up, meanwhile emotions are heightened, prides are heated up and intensified, reputation is tested, power is manifested, and wealth is flaunted. By now the blood runs hot in the bidder's veins, each one trying hard to bid higher to win the item and save face, and come out successfully out of the crowd.

Many people love to flaunt their power, fame, or wealth. Parading these phenomena is considered a kind of fulfillment, as if extinguishing their psychological thirst. Paris Hilton spent $325,000 on a doghouse to show her superiority that she could spend such a mint for a dog.

Passion will take you where she desires; wisdom will take you where you desire; therefore, listen to your wisdom to show you the right path, the right feeling, the proprieties.

14

WHAT IS THE HEART OF BUSINESS?

Have you thought of the heart of business? What do you think the heart of business is? Profit, reputation, compatible bargain, competitive deals, success and opportunity? These are alluring terms to introduce and define the business a great deal, but they will not pass muster as the heart of the business, the ideal that we always cherish and look after. When we deal with a business, what do we search about? Won't we search if the business is reliable, if it is not a scum, if it has a clean record? Definitely, these concepts are the very first that come to our minds. As a matter of fact, integrity is the heart of the business.

Unless you have been exposed to fraud by some business, you may not think much of its honesty, but once you are exposed to fraud, you know that it is so important that integrity is really the heart of business. Will you deal again with a business that has robbed you once? I do not think so.

A business that has no honesty, in fact, has no heart; then how can it survive? In the first place, it may not survive if its dishonesty is exposed because nobody will trust it; therefore, nobody will make business with it, although it may have already made a fortune. In the second place, even if it survives despite its dishonesty—by appealing to the simpleminded, unaware, disoriented, and even the honest people, and by sharpening its deceptive rhetoric—it proves to be just like a husband or wife who are unfaithful to each other, or an individual with no conscience, or a criminal at large, or a person who is walking into the unknown without cognizant of his or her destination.

Dishonesty surfaces in a multitude of forms and ways: being dishonest to yourself, to your family, to your society, and to your business. Dishonesty in business is the most egregious of all because of spawning fraud on a large scale, taking advantage of a great number of people in the form of business. Dishonest business kingpins transgress not only against their own souls but also against other sources such as their partners, clients, investors, and against society on the whole.

There are a number of motives that ignites and cultivates dishonesty in people. Greed, bad habit, success and opportunity, peer pressures, financial pressure, and an amalgamation of different motives are a few examples that have been ubiquitous. Greed is an egregious stimulant tempting the business kingpins to commit crimes. Greed in business indicates an insatiable lust for money, a lust to pile up money in heaps, no matter how. The more it is amassed, the more it is wanted. In fact, greed turns the kingpins into a Korah. Habit is also another addict that drives people into fraud. Bad habits can burgeon any time depending on the situation. The more loose, vain, undisciplined, or unprincipled they are, the more prone they are to bad habits. Mostly bad habits burgeon inside families who are loose, lax, and irresponsible. Peers and partners could also be remarkable influencers to adopt bad habits. Availing success and opportunity in order to be endowed with the comfort of life is everybody's appetite, which is a common fact. However, this appetite is so ravenous for some people that they assume great risk, retribution, and ignobility to take advantage of it. Sometimes financial pressures are also a good stimulus to commit fraud. There might be other causes or a combination of above-mentioned things that tempt people to adulterate their business with fraud and dishonesty.

To shake off dishonesty is an important decision—a real victory—in life. Efforts should be made that no shadow of it should be left behind. Why should we get rid of it? There are good enough reasons to abandon dishonesty. Having peace of mind is a very good reason to leave dishonesty, to connect to what is really ours, to be satisfied with what we have and proud of what we are. If we want to add to our comfort, we should feed on our own efforts, not others'. This is a straight way, a safe way, a noble way, and a humane way. By being honest, besides enjoying peace of mind, we enjoy a clean conscience, lofty soul, and beautiful heart. It is great to live worry-free and clean. We will enjoy life truly, decently, and to the full extent when there is no fear of being caught, arrested, despised, disrespected, unsecure, and guilty. In fact, we feel free. Explore your shadows, open your real self, and change yourself for better.

Honesty is not used only in business. Honesty should be planted in every child, every man, every woman, every house, every society, every situation, every action, every habit, every career, every craft, and whoever and whatever you are—if you be a father, a mother, a nurse, a teacher, a politician, a judge, a religious leader, a lawyer, a doctor, a scientist, a writer, a police officer, a military officer, a soldier, an anchorperson, a historian, a comedian, a star, an artist, a musician, a shopkeeper, an astronaut, a builder, a baker, a boatman, an athlete, a carpenter, a clerk, an artist, an engineer, an architect, a forester, a farmer, a journalist, a librarian, a driver, a pilot, etc. I am emphasizing honesty because it is the truth, a universal quality, the wide way, the bright way, the way from which you can never be lost. It is through honesty that you see your true self, a true replica of what you are: a magnificent exploration.

15

CREATIVE MINDS

Creativity means the ability to create an original or novel idea or product of any forms and patterns of value to be used, enjoyed, and appreciated. It can be literary, artistic, scientific, intellectual, etc. Creative minds exploit all kinds of sources and resources: visible and external, invisible and cognitive to create their ideal phenomena.

Creative minds stay ahead of the time, thinking bright, and visioning farther away; commonplace minds stay behind the time, being stunned by the typical dilemmas, and following a narrow vision. Creative minds exert themselves to overcome the hurdles, outwitting and outpacing their masters and superiors, and being fascinated only by the extraordinary; commonplace minds are fascinated by the ordinary and their superiors, yielding to them impetuously, and being impressed by them. Creative minds go deeper and deeper where there is unsought, unmarked, unbeaten, and untracked; commonplace minds always follow the existing tracks and marks.

To enjoy creativity, we do not need to owe it only to our innate power. Creativity can be acquired and nourished in the course of life. As Thomas Edison said, "Genius: one percent inspiration and 99 percent perspiration." Likewise, Albert Einstein's achievements could not be attributed only to his brain, but to his diligence, his research, and the way he used his intelligence. As a matter of fact, we can think creatively, act creatively, behave creatively, and live creatively. By acting or behaving creatively, I do not mean to outdo others in bad behavior, but instead, excel them in good behavior.

It is indispensable to create appropriate conditions for creativity to grow. As growth and activity suit the nature of creativity, inactivity and torpidity will sap its stamina. Therefore, conditions to enhance such growth are vital, so that creative people should keep abreast of their aspiring needs and dreams. To keep this growth going, the following conditions are worthy of consideration:

First, proper conditions are necessary to accommodate the creative minds for the best possible results. Proper conditions allude to the fact that creative people are socially, politically, educationally, and psychologically comfortable, that their efforts are encouraged by a cooperative and trustworthy environment, and that their works are appreciated. The more resources they will be bestowed with, the more they may benefit from their creative mind. The better these conditions, the better their yields. That is why wherever those conditions and opportunities have been fostered there inventions and discoveries have been much more lavish than any other place where these conditions have been denied. It is also true that when a discovery or an invention has emerged in a community, it has stimulated other creative minds to think of similar ideas and products. That is, in a community, some inventions and discoveries have induced other inventions and discoveries.

Second, creative minds need to be free, feel free, think free, and, to a great extent, problem free. These freedoms will contribute a lot to the expansion of creativity. Creative minds may be prepared and honed to solve problems, but do not think of them as invincible as Hercules. In fact, problem solving is different from resisting or tolerating a problem. Therefore, think of them as being innovative and inspired, not Herculean.

Third, creative minds should be encouraged to step up their self-confidence. They can be encouraged in different ways. For example, if their discoveries and inventions need financial support, opportunities to fend off their needs must be created. Even If the inventors make little of their ideas will prove to be better than facing a cul-de-sac to avail nothing. This support is in relation to some inventions or discoveries that involve financial dilemmas and their inventors to get such support are at their wits' end. I myself am one of these guys. Thus, the inventors not only need motivation but also economical support if their ideas are utilitarian and worthwhile.

Fourth, creative minds must be persevere, determined, and energetic in order to be effective and useful. In fact, their success comes mostly from their perspiration rather than their inspiration. At times it may arise that creative minds will face frustrating barriers; therefore, they need to be determined enough to negotiate the obstacles and pave their ways for success.

Fifth, at the present time, entrepreneurship is an integral part of creative minds. In the absence of professional business plans, their idea might fail or will not yield the proper results anticipated. Such people as Thomas Edison and Bill Gates made the best out of their creativity for availing themselves of entrepreneurism.

16

THE TWO UNIVERSAL CULTURES

There are two universal cultures—culture of the humanity, culture of the Devil.

Humans are born with the culture of humanity—culture that is worthy of humankind, belongs to humankind, celebrated by humankind, and should proudly be preserved by humankind. It is culture of respect, of love, of care, of friendship, of harmony and peace, of humbleness, of modesty, of simplicity, of order, of righteousness, of virtue, of justice, of goodness, of truth, of optimism, of hope, of growth, of faith, of lofty aspirations, of success, of security, of intellect, of understanding, etc.

Culture of the Devil is that of inhumanity, of hatred, of animosity, of partiality, of ignorance, of inequity, of hopelessness, of insecurity, of temptation, of falsehood, of deception, of sin, of vanity, of conceit, of confusion, of mayhem, of miseries, of cynicism, of lust, of tyranny, of transgression, of frustration, of devastation, etc.

When the two cultures mingled human legacies were sabotaged regretfully. The bitter irony is that the culture of the devil has not been affected by such acculturation, nor has it improved, nor has it worsened, because it has already been in its worst state, in the depth of darkness, which overshadows all other darkness. This cultural mingling proves to mark the most egregious incident in the history of humankind. While culture of the Devil has remained viciously intact, human culture has vindictively and notoriously been affected and adulterated. Humanity has been intruded and vitiated by the Devil and his incursions so much so that the former has virtually lost its identity. Thus, human beings have been influenced by the opposite culture, having lived with it side by side, grown with it; their lives have been assaulted left and right, their actions dehumanized, their habits polluted, their emotions fermented, their minds affected, their souls weakened and dominated, and thus humanity has turned into a shambles. Under these difficult conditions, humans—without cognizance of their real enemy, in the name of race, color, nationality, religion, language, caste and class, rank, etc.—have been set against each other to fight, to oppress, to be filled with revenge, to abuse, to exploit, to transgress each other's rights, so that they have become so torn apart that as if they are creatures of two different worlds.

To get rid of this dire situation, human beings have to purify and rescue their culture by recognizing their true and acknowledged enemy to live in peace, prosperity, happiness, and to enjoy and live a life worthy of theirs.

17

IS THE CONSPIRING SERPENT FORGIVABLE?

Hearing of the conspiring Serpent, won't you recall the story of Eve, who was deceived by Satan to eat from the prohibited tree? According to this story, Satan morphed into a serpent to change his identity to delude Eve into the dire snare. Adam was also deluded by Eve to commit the sin, and therefore they were expelled from the paradise.

Forgiveness is sacred, magnanimous, human, and great. Yet, is everybody pardonable for all atrocities and sins?

One thing should be mentioned that those criminals who transgress against humanity and will be punished by law assume that by serving their sentence will pay off their crime; therefore, there is no need to ask for forgiveness. There might be a number of conditions: the victim might have lost his or her life, which may obviate the condition for forgiveness. That is, how can the perpetrator communicate with the dead victim to ask for forgiveness? Some criminals might be at large, going into hiding for the rest of their lives with different identities to mislead the law. Or a perpetrator can be a serial killer or a serial rapist whose case is too extraordinary and complex to come under forgiveness, etc.

Let's first clear: who is seeking forgiveness, and who is the giver? Experiences have proven that those who are seeking forgiveness can be categorized into several groups. However, in order to make the discussion clear and simple, let's classify them into three distinct groups: one, pardonable; two, unpardonable; three, conditional.

First, the pardonable group is those who have committed sin but have acknowledged their misdeeds and regretted. Further, they have come to the realization that there is an absolute, universal justification for every deed, or for every cause there is an effect. Their misdeeds could be both deliberate and impulsive. Besides feeling contrite, they feel uneasy, and they wish to get rid of their sin weighing upon them as a burden. In fact, their conscience has affected them to the extent that they feel the burden is always present and convincing.

Second, the unpardonable group is those who have committed a number of atrocities both severe and mild. They have not confessed their sins, nor have they regretted, and nor are they prepared to confess or regret. They are still ready to continue to their wrongdoings. They believe in no justification; they have committed wrongs deliberately, without feeling any burden on their shoulders, without feeling uneasiness of conscience, or any kinds of contrition. In fact, they do not believe in any justification. That is, they believe the end of those who have been good and charitable is the same as those who have been wicked and unconscientious. Simply, ultimate reward or punishment is of no significance for them. Thus, they are determined in what they believe; therefore, they are not expected to change their mind until they die. They think they have come to live by chance without any divine intervention and significance, and so they depart from the world without any consequences, without any accountability, without any justification. In fact, their death will put an end to all their misdeeds.

The third group is those who have committed misdeeds, and they still continue to commit; however, they are wavering between stopping and continuing their perpetration. They are neither determined to continue their mischievous activities, nor are they apt to stop them. As amateur wrongdoers, they commit wrong here and there, and they also favor people when they are in a good mood. They are of two minds, and they are mostly following their emotion rather than their mind. As a matter of fact, this group will get the attention of forgivers only when they come to their senses, acknowledging their sins, and exhorting their victims' pardon.

In the light of what has been proven, it is clear that those who are seeking forgiveness have been rich, powerful, high profile, arrogant, charismatic, pompous, ambitious, high-handed, motivated, pretentious, and crafty. These characteristics have been apt to abuse—the powerful taking advantage of their power, the high-profile individuals paving their way for self-interest, the arrogant hurting the underprivileged, the high-handed people leaving their subordinates out, the pompous and ambitious grasping all the opportunities for themselves to enjoy, and the corrupt transgressing vehemently whenever they can, the rogues flaunting their opportunities and resources, and the crafty building their snares. Thus, the powerful, the oppressors, the abusers, and the arrogant could be easily manipulated to dance to the devil's tune.

Now let's see who the forgivers are: they are innocent, poor, underprivileged, subordinate, weak, ordinary, unmotivated, and simple—characteristics that are least prone to temptation.

Therefore, they are not in a position to transgress, to corrupt, to encroach upon others' rights, to dehumanize people, to flaunt their assets, to rob, to insult, to hurt others' feelings, to behave in a haughty way, or to walk condescendingly, because they lack the opportunities for such commitments. Therefore, they owe no one anything; therefore, they need not exhort anybody for forgiveness.

Who is the beguiling, conspiring Serpent? Isn't it the devil that conspired against Eve, resulting in her own and her spouse's expulsion from the Garden of Eden? Although she disobeyed God, will she be forgivable? The answer is in the positive because she was, to her long-life regret, deceived. Is her conspiring serpent forgivable? Is the serial killer who has committed many cold-blooded murders forgivable? Is the child molester who has built his pleasure upon the miseries of children forgivable? Is the rapist who has devastated many lives forgivable? Is the tyrant who has committed crimes against humanity forgivable? Is the wealthy man who has stripped the people of their fortune forgivable? Is the criminal who has built his life upon fraud forgivable? Is the villain who has lived upon others' misfortune forgivable? Is the evil one whose corruption has spread out far and beyond forgivable? These are that Serpent or the accomplices of the Serpent transgressed against humanity, who have not come to their senses, who have not acknowledged their sins, and who have not resented.

18

VISIBLE AND INVISIBLE PHENOMENON

Nature is endowed with two types of configurations—visible and invisible. Visible configuration concerns itself with all those natural phenomena that are capable of being seen and sought. Invisible configuration concerns itself with natural laws that work behind the curtain, laws whose understanding involves perspicacity and knowledge, as it is generally hard to understand them.

Nature is bound by these codes and configurations because they are its integral part; in their absence nature ceases to exist. These two codes are applied to nature either externally or internally. Laws of nature such as gravity and electromagnetism, for example, are internal laws—laws that function invisibly. Other features of nature, such as growth, evaporation, and liquefaction, raining, snowing, lightening, shining, are visible and external activities. Similarly, it is related to the internal characteristics of certain species to live in water, or on land, or to fly. In the same manner, certain birds have a unique aptitude to build nests, and certain animals have the capacity to change their color when confronting a predator. Certain species may also live in both water and on land, given their innate characteristics. Such aptitudes are true of other plants and animals and even of the whole species.

19

DO WE LIVE IN HARMONY OR IN CONFUSION?

At first glance, this question will startle anyone. This is also true of a credo, a rite, or a traditional aspect being disputed, because each one of which is so deeply rooted in our life that it is assimilated into our character, that it has become a part of our personality, so that only a cogent reasoning, a broader enlightenment will initiate us into a change.

As I understand, there are two kinds of harmonies—physical and moral. Physical harmony embodies the entire universe, from the smallest bits to the biggest heavenly bodies—harmony in atomic and subatomic particles, harmony among the planets and stars, harmony in the shapes. Look at animals and human beings. How beautifully and symmetrically they are shaped from both within and without, from top to bottom. How their organs function in perfect harmony.

By moral harmony, it is understood that we should use our entire mental and emotional qualities, capacities, and tendencies properly and reasonably. In other words, our personality should be so harmoniously intact and protected that nothing can fail it. For instance, one's power shouldn't be abused; one's knowledge will benefit others; if there is no reason involved, one should refrain from hurting others physically or emotionally; or it is proper that a person be inculcated with mercy and forbearance and affection, etc.

Similarly, there are two kinds of chaos—physical and moral. Physical chaos can be prompted socially, politically, naturally, involving as simple as a daily encounter occurring within oneself or one's family, or a more serious chaotic situation happening in a party, in a community, in a malfunctioned device such as antenna, in a malfunctioned organ such as a heart, or more complex phenomenon happening due to a climatic turmoil, or worse than that, a more complicated one such as a state of things controlled by chance and unpredictability, or the confused state of primordial matter before the creation of distinct forms following the big bang.

Moral confusion seems to be the opposite of moral harmony. In moral or spiritual harmony human personality is characterized in such harmony so that all the deteriorating, destructive, negative, or corrupt qualities and tendencies should be kept in bay. But in a moral chaos our personality is given to wickedness, injustice, oppression, jealousy, rancor, dishonesty, lies, and other immoral behavior; therefore, other pervert qualities will be assimilated into our character.

Now that we are acquainted with both moral and physical harmony and chaos, and they are well defined, my necessity of coping with the theme of this article makes me elaborate what morality or spirituality actually means. Morality or spirituality to a good number of people sounds like the sound of a drum from a distance and nothing more. I mean they think of it very vainly, insignificantly, and inconsequentially. They think it has only verbal or virtual or imaginary significance, not practical. In other words, it doesn't pay. Morality is a manifestation of harmony.

When we say something is in harmony, we mean it is in its best possible state. For example, when we say someone is healthy, in fact, we mean he or she is healthy physically, mentally, morally, and psychologically. A person who is morally and psychologically unhealthy cannot be healthy, because he or she lacks a harmonious life. As harmony is a manifestation of good, beauty, and perfection, morality, in the same way, embellishes one's personality with good and beauty, and leads it toward refinement.

Nowadays morality is out of style, for people say that it doesn't have a tangible value. But it does pay. It pays heavily. Morality is priceless and protecting it from corruption is the most ideal endeavor. Nothing is more gifted than this, and therefore, nothing should shatter its sanctity. It pays pricelessly and in multiple ways. The way it pays is easy, simple, and pure. Let's think of a conqueror, who in order to conquer, will undergo a lot of physical and mental scenes and scenarios involving an array of thoughts, plans, technology, techniques, tactics, time, money, lives, destructions, devastations, damages, misfortunes, miseries, etc. In fact, this conqueror has played a gamble risking his own life and others'. If he loses, his loss is immense and irreparable. If he wins, his victory will be transient, not ultimate, for it involves critical spiritual and moral drawbacks. I did cite an example of the secular conqueror. Now I gave an example of a spiritual conqueror, whose victory, unlike the former, involves no military campaigns or plans, no mobilizations, no marshal strategies, no technologies, no techniques, no tactics, no soldiers, no money, no destructions, no devastations, no misery, no loss, no hustle and bustle, who tries to conquer his desires, rein in his unbridled temptations, and harmonize his emotions. This is a real victory, a victory which lasts forever, a spiritual victory. This individual won't rob, nor will he extort, nor will he bribe, nor will he rape, nor will he kill, nor will he harm anybody, nor will he deceive, nor will he be a threat to anybody or anybody's rights and property, nor will he oppress or suppress, nor will he insult or slur anybody. He will live in peace and harmony, with dignity, and will honor all measures, statutes, and denominations of humanity. He needs no courts, no jails, no penitentiaries, for his beautiful conscience will be his supreme court, and he is confident to remain immaculate. Likewise, he needs no law enforcement, because he is incapable of doing wrongs. He needs no security officers, no guards, for his motto is peace, understanding, and transparency. As he doesn't steal and is inoffensive, houses, shops, malls, and supermarkets can survive unguarded, unprotected, carefree. Spiritually, this individual will be a token of peace, honesty, and tranquility; materially, a great asset for the human society, where poverty will be attacked vigorously. Thus, an immaculate culture will be encouraged and created, which is worthy of mankind—this is a gift from spirituality and morality.

20

WHAT IS FAITH?

Faith is a strong tree stemming from God. It is a formidable house whose light comes from God. It is a light whose fuel is provided by God. Therefore, faith is a safe haven whose rope is strong, secure, and promising to hold on to.

When you claim that you are people of faith, you have actually appealed to a security free of any reservations and harm. The stronger your belief in faith, the more sure-footed and strong you feel, and you will enjoy the safe house, the prolific tree.

Thus real faith comes from God, giving you a sense of peace, security, and delight. The more you believe in God, the stronger your faith is; the more you know Him, the more formidable is your understanding and recognition of God.

The tree of faith can be grown in every soul. The more you nourish it, the more it will grow. You can enlarge the house of faith within yourselves, and so can you brighten the light of faith as much as you wish.

21

A FORESIGHT OF 2019

With few exceptions, 2019 will be more or less the cousin of 2018, in particular, socially, politically, and economically. Technologically, to be sure, the coming year will be much more advanced than the year before. The fact that my focus is much more on technology is because of its vital role in society, creating a clear distinction between today and yesterday. Recently, technology has gone so far that people are looking forward to enjoying their trips down under the sea or up in the space, searching for another planet to occupy, hunting for the wormholes to make way for distant spaces and planets, and trying to use centrifugal force to lift water from the low to the higher levels.

In spite of technological factors that are always in progress, social, political, and economical phenomena could be trending up or down, regardless of the passage of time. The giant of technology is growing faster and faster time after time, while economical status is unpredictable, or predictably, more inclined to a slow-down trend. However, there are grounds for optimism to hope that technological progress may direct the economy to the direction whereby windows of opportunities may open upon the common folk to keep the heat of their summers and the cold of their winters at bay. How so? If free energy, which still suffers from the suppression of the lords of energy and interest groups, becomes available to the public, humanity will be surprised with a tremendous change: clean energy will replace carbon fuel, and our environment will be freed from the pollution, which is a major threat to our health; salt water will be changed into fresh water, whereby dry lands will be cultivated, and communities supplied with healthy drinking water, triggering food abundance, eliminating shortage of energy, and many other changes will come to pass.

Clean energy, which is called renewable or off-the-grade, comes from two kinds of sources: one is coming from natural sources such as sun, wind, water, and biomass, whose usage requires funds, depending on the size, type, and quality of the service. The other kind of energy that costs little comes from perpetual motion machines, cold fusion generators, and torus-based generators, which work perpetually without any fuel such as gas, petroleum, and suchlike fuels, depending on mechanical systems, and once they are available, the key to put them in motion is in our hands, and they can be used without fossil fuel, water, wind, and sun.

Despite the fact that these sources of energy have been at our disposal, we have been using coal, oil, and natural gas to supply our energy. Indeed, it is the scheme of the greedy interest groups burdened on us. However, sooner or later environmental pressure forces humanity to shift away from fossils to renewable energy. This pressure comes from two viable angels: First, it has been predicted that carbon fuel is subject to depletion in the passage of time; therefore, people have to turn to renewable energy. Second, our environment has already been polluted with greenhouse gasses—a major threat to public health. Thus, shortage of energy, food, fresh air, and freshwater are good reasons to turn to dispose of carbon fuel and turn to the technology producing pollution-free, profuse energy for everybody, everywhere.

To live healthily and comfortably, human communities should be acquainted with free energy, and the way should be paved to utilize it. It is through wisdom, sharing, caring, cooperation, and humanity that people could enjoy wealth and abundance, could overcome their fears and problems, live in peace, and enjoy a livable environment, not through nonsense, conflict, tension, and mistrust.

22

IS TIME VALUABLE FOR ALL?

Time is a free commodity that everyone enjoys universally. Time has been deemed to be the most valuable thing, but its value depends on how it is used. In fact, the times of the honored, the comfortable, the fortunate, and the successful are different from those of the miserable, the unlucky, and the hopeless. Those who are indulging themselves with a good time, and they are using it happily, time proves to be very valuable for them. On the contrary, for those who cannot invest in it or use it properly, time seems to be the cheapest commodity for them. For example, for those whose lives prove to be a burden for them, time could even be such a misery that they are anxious to get rid of it. Such is the times of the sick, the poor, the unfortunate, and the afflicted. Thus, the value of the time is proportionate to how it is used. Those who are able to exploit the time, it is valuable, but the cheapest commodity for those who waste it.

23

TWO KINDS OF IDs

Humans are identified with two kinds of identifications: internal and external. External ID is verifying name, business, whereabouts, connections, including social, political, educational information, and such. This ID is temporary. It could be subject to change and circumstances during lifetime. Internal ID covers hidden, deep, unknown, and unexpected phenomena, including spiritual, moral, ethical characteristics and thoughts This ID is a permanent position of a person, being as eternal as the spirit of the person, remaining beyond time, bodily, and worldly relationships and concerns, without being lost, altered, denied, added to, or reduced from.

24

TWO KINDS OF CHANGES

To define the change, it should be elaborated that there are two kinds of changes: positive and negative. Positive change will improve life, facilitate life, and make it comfortable. Of course, this change will include moral and ethical change, for example, ameliorating relations between individuals and societies; facilitating distribution of wealth to the entire humanity fairly; finding ways to break down the wall of prejudices and injustice, just to mention a few. Negative change will include moral and ethical deterioration; political corruption; growth of greed, mistrust, jealousy, self-indulgence; proliferation of chemical, biological, and technological weapons that will annihilate human race summarily, to mention a few. What will be the definition of a change if it brings destruction and corruption? What will be the definition of a change if it gives rise to greed, jealousy, and prejudices? Thus, we should be prepared for a race against time to save our ship and humanity from being sunk.

25

RELY IN THE ALMIGHTY

When you know a mayor, you may pride yourself on his friendship. If you know a governor, you may even take pleasure in his acquaintance. If you know a president, or a king, or preferably you are familiar with an emperor, you will feel exuberant, protected, ingratiating yourself with all those celebs and powerful people. After all, it is only a matter of time before all this glory goes to glory, all your pride goes before a fall, and you will be left vulnerable, as if you have been wishing for the spiderwebbed house. Best of all, why not aspire to implore the Almighty's favor, Who is king of all kings, power of all powers, helper of anyone who needs help, provider of all provisions, protector of all the vulnerable, source of all happiness, honors, and fulfillments? Who can protect you deep in the ground, where nobody can reach? Who can help you deep in the ocean, where nobody can find you? Who can help you if you are precariously stuck at the heights where human assistance is not disposable? Of course, God, Whose support is always free, always available, reliable, infinite, and ubiquitous.

26

CARAVAN OF HUMAN EXPERIENCES

Across the history of humanity, human experiences have been stored, collected, and passed onto future generations through oral and written language plus artistic phenomenon. Orally, these experiences have been transferred from one mouth to another, which in the meantime have been added to or subtracted from tremendously. In the beginning, these experiences have been very short and primitive, but along language development, phenomenal changes have occurred. Written experiences, given its complexity, have been more systematic, having undergone much more intricacies than oral phenomena. In the beginning, these experiences have been presented by drawings, but in the course of written language development, drawings phenomena have been accompanied or replaced by alphabetical language. Written language has been plodding wearily through extensive slow development until the printing press was invented by Gutenberg, whereby handwritten documents fell in the hands of printers, entailing a revolution in book publishing. Later on, phenomenal commercial printers and media services developed, which have created enormous facilities to distribute human knowledge and experiences with much more accuracy and speed globally. Present technological development pioneered cutting-edge techniques whereby oral and written language has gone through such a phenomenal development that years of work of antiquity could be reduced into a few moments of work of the present.

27

PATIENCE IS NOT JUST A VIRTUE BUT ALSO A NECESSITY

Some time ago, I was shopping for groceries and people were in line for checking out. One of the shoppers had difficulty paying his purchase. His credit card declined, and his cash could not cover the purchase, and as a result, delay was created. One of the shoppers objected to this disruption, and his contentious behavior led to first argument and then to fistfight, necessitating the immediate involvement of security guard in the first place, and that of police, in the second place. Such incidents I have witnessed that have happened from time to time anywhere, anytime, induce mild to severe consequences, and could have been avoided through a little patience. Thus, patience is not only a virtue but also an absolute necessity saving time, troubles, and tantrums. The same is true of other virtues that their efficacy is latent but of the essence.

28

FANATICISM

Fanaticism is a state of narrow-mindedness dealing with excessive devotion and passion in something. There are many kinds of fanaticism, all inducing subversive and negative consequences. Religious fanatics bring about mayhems, committing perpetrations that cannot make sense, their misdeeds appearing to be good, holy, and immaculate for them. This is because they are so much under the impression of their erratic opinions that they cannot differentiate wrong from right, good from bad. Political fanatics are appealing to all kinds of ways and means to grasp the helm of power. Once they get the power, they try to keep it perpetually, forcing their ideas on others, no matter how many lives are jeopardized and lost, how many cities are destroyed, and how much assets are wasted. Political fanatics push on using their power; religious fanatics push on using their belief. Financial fanaticism leads to greed and usury. Financial fanatics are running by their own interest and passion, using all kinds of means to arrive at their purpose, unmindful of their moral and ethical values, and devaluing their conscience. Social fanaticism involves excessive love of fame, rank, and wealth. Social fanatics try to climb the highest ladder of the society to secure their personal caprices. Among all other fanaticism, there is also athletic fanaticism, which involves hero-worshiping well-known players and excessive love of certain sports.

29

STILL NOT TOO LATE

We are living in an era when sexy, sinister, dark stories, despite their negative outcome and impressions, are much more heeded and signified than moral, spiritual, or ethical facts of life. Is it because the older generations have left their posterity without moral injunctions and words of wisdom? Is it because depth is superseded by superficialities? Is it because evil is more strengthening and getting the better of good? Not so. In fact, people are influenced by evil, which is feeding on weakness, misery, and corruption. Perhaps a touch of all those phenomena might contribute to making bad choices. Still not too late in an effort to build the foundation of our children with such faith, truth, and humanity that not only they themselves will hold firmly to those values, but they may also transfer those values to their own offspring. The sooner the present generation takes that step, the better.

30

Diversity in Creativity

Creativity is a magical touch to be applied in all things. Our minds, our imaginations, our sights, our tastes, our hearings, and all our senses and faculties should be inclusive of creative perspective. Nature is a garden full of colors, diversities, wonders, wealth, and means perfused by all kinds of qualities, shapes, sizes, characteristics, and dimensions. All these are phenomenal things to sharpen our imagination and inspire us with profuse perspective and vision.

The other day, my son ordered food from outside. It was so tasteless that I avoided eating it. Or I have found certain processed food such as cereals, cookies, bread etc., very flavorless. Even there are manufactured products that have been made defective, houses that have been built in an ugly manner, and many plans have gone wrong now and again. I have noticed in offices and the workplace whose plans and procedures have been flawed. These have been a few examples that have been mentioned here. There are a multitude of other things that are sharing the same fate. All of them have been lacking in creativity. If those in charge had put some taste and creativity in their products, the food would have been tasty, the utensils flawless, the houses beautiful, and the offices' plans and works would have been much satisfactorily improved.

Of course, prodigy and gifted talent cannot be ignored, and the genius of such people as Ibni Sina, Michael Angelo, Tesla, Newton, Einstein and such other geniuses will always be remembered. However, as Edison says, genius is 1 percent inspiration and 99 percent perspiration, hard work, patience, fortitude, care, and attention are ingredients of making genius, in whose absence, genius will fade away.

It is not wise to think that creativity belongs to a single trade, trend, or craft. For example, it belongs to an artist who is capable of creating art, or to a writer who creates stories, or to an inventor who has invented something, or to a discoverer who is author of a discovery. There are two ways that creativity is considered in this article. To be creative, you don't have to be a writer, or an artist, or an inventor. Everyone who is capable of thinking and is the owner of faculties could be creative. It is one way of thinking into creativity. A different way of thinking of creativity is to be creative not only in a single phenomenon, but you have to be creative in all things. I mean you have to be creative in what you cook, what you make, what you write, what you do, what you think, what you plan, what you solve, what you sculpt, what you paint, what you craft, what you plant, what you choose, what you play, what you perform, and a host of other things.

I am convinced that creativity like many other things may need the right conditions and opportunity to give results. Too many geniuses have had forfeited that opportunity. Therefore, their gifted talent has been nipped in the bud, without having the chance to grow and fructify it. As a matter of fact, it is imperative for parents to discover their talented children and provide them with the right conditions to develop their genius. Teachers, trainers, coaches, mentors, or other elements who are dealing with gifted children should do their best to pave the way for children to grow their flair properly.

31

INNOVATION SHOULD BE A MEANS OF EASE

Recently, I lost a bunch of texts from my iPhone without my knowledge, or my long texts have been omitted by a slight touch or fidget. These things have happened to many other product users, too. Innovations should make things comfortable, not sensitive to the extent of losing one's efforts.

Sometimes, today's technology in order to bring variations and changes to update their products such as iPhone, to make a pretense of innovations and development, are venturing into such incautious measures that things are complicated instead of being facilitated. One small example of their incautiousness is putting *cut* and *copy* together when copying a text, and when you are writing a text a slight touch might cut your text, without giving you a chance to retrieve it. Or your texts are disappearing from your iPhone without one's knowledge. These things are changes that do not make things easy. Innovations should make things comfortable, not sensitive to the extent of losing one's efforts. They should be very cautious with what they are doing. Their change should bring comfort and facilities, not disappointment.

32

THE OPPOSITES

Life is made from pairs of opposites. Truth and untruth, good and bad, light and dark, sweet and bitter, happiness and sadness, cold and heat, hard and soft, rough and smooth.

While we see visible things such as light and dark, big and small, wide and narrow, low and high, or things related to our senses such as bitter and sweet, happiness and sadness, low and high. However, it has happened repeatedly that people have not known good from bad, truth from untruth, honor and dignity from ignobility. While those qualities and characteristics that build our personality are so weak and corrupt that as if people are living under a roof whose walls are founded upon the sand.

Things that are related to senses are not difficult to be distinguished and known from one another. For example, it is easy to know hard from soft, smooth from rough, short from long, bitter from sweet, quiet from noise. However, cognitive things are affected by subjectivity, objectivity, volition, and discretion, emotion, level of understanding, and other ways and means. That is why distinction between good and evil, just and unjust, right and wrong, truth and untruth turn to be controversial.

There are a number of different approaches toward good and evil, right and wrong, truth and untruth: people who truly know those concepts, distinguishing one from another with certainty, and intending to be discreet with their choice. An example of this group is the prophets. Contrarily, people who are ignorant about those concepts, embracing or denying them as far as their conditions allow. An example of this group is fanatics of all kinds. There are also those who are mindless about those concepts, dicing with them carelessly, accepting them indiscriminately, and indulging in what that pleases them. An example of this group is the criminals. And finally, there are those who are a blend of all those groups, whether they are common or elite, educated or uneducated, poor or rich.

33

NATURAL RESOURCES

All the natural resources in a country belong to each and every citizen of that country. Citizens should avail themselves of these resources either directly or indirectly. Directly, either they have a fair share in these resources per se, or in terms of value, their equivalent cash. Indirectly, the resources should be built into quality establishments and services to serve all. The resources should preferably be of service to the disadvantaged, the disabled, and the needy more than others. Those who take advantage of these natural resources by transgressing the limits are payable to the rest of the citizens and accountable to God.

34

LEADERSHIP

Pilots are at the helm of their ships, so are leaders entirely at the helm of their countries, unlike those who are at the helm of their own lives. Here I am concerned only with the highest-ranking political leaders who are presiding over their countries, who have been rulers, who have been titled in the course of history as pharos, Caesars, czars, emperors, ameers, sultans, kings, queens, dukes, rajahs, shahs; and recent leadership titles as presidents and prime ministers. Leaders' failure reflects their countries' failure; leaders' success resonates their countries' success. What weighs down leadership's burden is this shared responsibility that cannot be avoided. Leadership cannot remain unheard of or unconcerned with injustices going on in their countries, violations of individuals' rights, violations of individuals' assets, all kinds of individuals' harms and damages that could be eliminated by the leadership. We have witnessed in the course of history that there have been a tremendous number of leaders who have proved to be a huge burden rather than of service to their people, and they have been useless and corrupt as dirt.

35

MISSION OF THE LEADERS

O leaders, whatever you are—a czar, an emperor, an ameer, a sultan, a king, a duke, a queen, a rajah, a president, or a prime minister—you are representing, leading, presiding over a nation or a community; therefore, you are not only running your own life, but also lives of the multitude. As a matter of fact, you have double responsibilities—responsibility against your own life and responsibility against lives of those you are in charge. You have been honored with these titles to bring peace, happiness, prosperity, and comfort for your people, making yourself useful, not just to enjoy your power and be a useless body. Leaders' failure reflects their countries' failure; leaders' success is their countries' success. What weighs down leadership burden is this shared responsibility that cannot be avoided. Leadership cannot remain unheard of or unconcerned with injustices going on in their countries, violations of individuals' rights, violations of individuals' assets, all kinds of individuals' harms and damages that could be eliminated by the leadership. God will bless you with your good deeds and convict you of your misdeeds.

36

IDIOCENTRISM

Human development across the recent technological breakthroughs has gone through a cautionary shift.

Day by day, while the giant of technology is towering over the human race, and the horse of progress is advancing at full gallop, integral human values such as spirituality, truth, family values, peace of mind, harmony, integrity, compassion, accountability, fortitude, patience, tolerance, and respect are paling into insignificance; individualism reduces to egotism, or to put it in better term, idiocentrism; collectivism changes into allocentrism; and human headway is resonated with rampant misgivings, lies, greed, and debauch. Although these breakthroughs emerge from the hands of the progressive human kind, the more they touch our lives, the more we confront the unexpected evils, losing time-honored values. In fact, we gain something, but instead, lose something, and, as a whole, the entire transaction comes to be subtle, intrinsic, deceptive, and dicey. To portray the situation realistically, humanity in the depth of the recent progress appears to be a building, which on the surface proves to be beautiful but within infested with mold, evoking the collapse of human coexistence.

37

GOOD WAYS, EVIL WAYS

Usually evil is committed when people fail to achieve something they desire. Pushing their will to realize their dreams, while blinded to the consequences, they are just walking against river currents. For example, if they need money, the shortest, though risky, way to get it is to steal. Or if they desire to enjoy power, they choose to fight to defeat their opponents. Or if they wish to enjoy a political or social position, they appeal to bribery, ingratiation, sycophancy, deception, lies, or selling their soul or body. Thus, evil ways are different from good ways. Evil ways involve risk, impatience, shortcut, damage, destruction, deception, corruption, and stupidity. Good ways are accompanied with wisdom, patience, hard work, good efforts, thinking, and planning. A good example, between a good and evil way is between building and demolishing a building, or between planting and rooting out a fruit tree.

38

WHO IS TO BLAME?

Once in a while, we finger times and ways of the world over our miseries and failures. The world has been established upon adequately logical principles. It will not treat us harshly unless we become harsh on ourselves. Usually, we wrong ourselves, or we are being wronged by others. In fact, humanity's system has been vitiated by humans' improper relationships time and time again. This relationship has always been so much at stake that human beings themselves have been the cause of each other's misfortune. Good relationships and understanding not only bring us peace and comfort but also economical success for all. Unmindful of our own evil ways, we find this and that accountable for unfavorable consequences.

39

THE MOMENT OF KNOWLEDGE

Knowledge is a light that lightens everything both internally and externally. When we have knowledge of something, we recognize it, and on the basis of our understanding we value it. If we know God, we glorify him. If we have knowledge of the world, we estimate it according to our understanding, not more, not less. If we have knowledge of ourselves, we apply for the missing qualities and avoid unfavorable ones. When God asked the angels to prostrate to Adam, Satan refused to obey God because he thought he was better than angels on the account that he is made from fire and Adam from the mud. Angels also disapproved of it, but God convinced them on the basis of knowledge. The Egyptian Pharaoh, who claimed to be a god, had no knowledge, neither of himself nor of the world. He had no knowledge of himself because he was deliberately arrogating to himself the status of divinity. And he had no knowledge of the world, because when Moses introduced the Almighty to him, he ordered his builder to build a tower to reach him to God. Therefore, he thought he was so close to the heavens that he could reach God by building him a tower. Thus true knowledge of something is important to be able to determine the true value of it. To know oneself is as important as a goldsmith's knowledge of gold. If a goldsmith lacks knowledge of gold, his business will be wrecked. True knowledge of oneself will prevail to recognize one's abilities, faculties, failures and success, and to drop what is excessive, add to what is short of. Thus, one will be prepared for life. Otherwise, he or she will be like a job seeker who applies for a job, with no or a little knowledge of it. People who are applying for leadership, should have a thorough understanding of what they are, who they are, what they can do, what they know, what they lack. Otherwise, like a goldsmith who has no knowledge of gold, they will give themselves up to failure.

40

MEANINGFULNESS VS. MEANINGLESSNESS

From the ground to the heavens, a panorama of multitude things are popping up before our eyes: small particles such as oxygen, which is only seeable in the sunrays; water; soil; rocks; foliage; plants; bushes; mountains; stars; planets; galaxies, etc. They are all meaningful. They are as meaningful as organs and systems in our bodies. All the things created naturally are ensuring a purpose, contributing to nature in some way. Thus, the whole creation is indicative of a purpose, and so is human creation as purposeful as body parts and systems. Even a building that falls down is significant if there is no evil attempt or conspiracy involved in it. Once, its collapse has been conspired by somebody, then its destruction becomes meaningless, for in the first instance, it may signify a purposeful fact such as wearing and tearing of the building, but in the second instance, its collapse has been resulted from an evil attempt. Now, despite human organs and systems, which have been created with ultimate meaning and purpose, human actions and decisions are either meaningful or meaningless, depending on the purpose they are completing. If their purpose is logical, their action is meaningful. If their purpose is illogical, their action is meaningless. We give meaning to, and we take meaning away from our life. We bless our life; we curse our life. We live either meaningfully, with purposeful strategies and ways, or we live meaninglessly, purposelessly, mindlessly. There are actions, thoughts, manners, relations, and trades that contribute to the significance of life. Likewise, there are actions, thoughts, manners, relations, and trades that take meaning away from life.

In proportion to this understanding, we also find such an arrangement between good and evil, wrong and right, falsity and truth.

41

AMBIGUITY OF THE UNIVERSAL TRAITS

There is a manifest difference between darkness and light, the blind and the seeing, and the deaf and hearing people. In fact, in those examples, gain and loss are visible and comprehensive. However, in many ways, distinction between such universal traits as good and evil, wrong and right, truth and falsehood, have been either obscured heedlessly or ignored categorically. The fact that a conscious understanding of good and evil has been undermined because evils have been committed indiscriminately, and so has falsehood been accepted frequently, and lies have been rampant humongously. The reason these qualities, despite their enormous significance, are not recognized properly to be guarded safely, is that their return is not immediate, that their consequences are hidden, that understanding their real nature and gravity is subtle, that a multitude of people do not take them seriously, and that they do not believe in them. However, those attributes are an absolute standard providing the people with the principles of life, which are as important as the foundation of life bringing meaning and significance to their life, perpetuating it, dignifying it, and justifying it.

42

What Is Time?

Time is the subtlest, most evasive, undefined phenomenon. Life is hanging on time, which is, in reality, acting like a hangman, whose rope is to strangle us eventually while ticking by. Enjoying not more than dual dimensions, past and future, its present, which seems to be spread out as vast as skies, is, in fact, as tiny as less than a hair diameter, or, in reality, it does not exist at all. What is true about time is that its future is fathomless, so much so that it extends immeasurably. The story about the future and past resembles a river, with two distinguished sides: one side is hidden, the other side open. Water flows from the hidden side, filling the other side. What is clear about these two is this: future is rolling out; the past is rolling up.